STOP! ...The Play

by David Spicer
from an original idea by John Schwab

samuelfrench.co.uk

FOR AMATEUR PRODUCTION ENQUIRIES

UNITED KINGDOM AND WORLD
EXCLUDING NORTH AMERICA
plays@samuelfrench.co.uk
020 7255 4302/01

Each title is subject to availability from Samuel French, depending upon country of performance.

Acting Editions

BORN TO PERFORM

Playscripts designed from the ground up to work the way you do in rehearsal, performance and study

---

Larger, clearer text for easier reading

Wider margins for notes

Performance features like character and props lists, sound and lighting cues, and more

---

+ CHOOSE A SIZE AND STYLE TO SUIT YOU

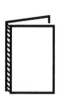

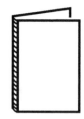

STANDARD EDITION

Our regular paperback book at our regular size

SPIRAL-BOUND EDITION

The same size as the Standard Edition, but with a sturdy, easy-to-fold, easy-to-hold spiral-bound spine

LARGE EDITION

A4 size and spiral bound, with larger text and a blank page for notes opposite every page of text. Perfect for technical and directing use

---

LEARN MORE | **samuelfrench.co.uk/actingeditions**

MUSIC USE NOTE

Licensees are solely responsible for obtaining formal written permission from copyright owners to use copyrighted music in the performance of this play and are strongly cautioned to do so. If no such permission is obtained by the licensee, then the licensee must use only original music that the licensee owns and controls. Licensees are solely responsible and liable for all music clearances and shall indemnify the copyright owners of the play(s) and their licensing agent, Samuel French, against any costs, expenses, losses and liabilities arising from the use of music by licensees. Please contact the appropriate music licensing authority in your territory for the rights to any incidental music.

ABOUT THE AUTHOR

David Spicer's stage plays include *Superheroes* (The King's Head, London and Edinburgh Festival), *Long Live the Mad Parade* (Ashcroft Theatre, Croydon) and *Raising Martha* (Park Theatre, London).

AUTHOR'S NOTE

The following script is the play as it was presented in London in 2015. The original idea that John Schwab and I worked on was to have as much fun as we possibly could with the nightmare rehearsals of an increasingly terrible play. And then, having made the characters suffer as much as we could, we decided to push the evening right over the edge and show the world's worst play in all its mad glory.

So what we ended up with was a full-length, two-hour play comprising two, very distinct acts, labelled here as REHEARSAL and PERFORMANCE. And whilst I definitely wouldn't recommend presenting the PERFORMANCE of our invented fellow playwright Hildred McCann's work to an audience without their first having seen how it came about, the REHEARSAL could well be presented to them as a one-act play in its own right.

At one point in REHEARSAL, Linda says she has an actor friend who does the voice of the Meerkat and could possibly get Gemma a "baby Oleg". This refers to a very popular advertising campaign that was running in Britain during the run of the play and always got a good response from the audience. However, as it is a topical reference, it can be changed with my permission and blessing to suit any time and place the play is staged.

However, whilst the references in PERFORMANCE to the rituals surrounding Saturday afternoon wrestling on the telly (which was an early and bizarre British precursor to WWE) may be equally obscure and baffling, I feel that they are just what Hildred would have wanted them to be.

David Spicer

Other plays by DAVID SPICER
published and licensed by Samuel French

Raising Martha

FIND PERFECT PLAYS TO PERFORM AT
www.samuelfrench.co.uk/perform

Stop! ...*The Play* was first produced by Tim Beckmann for Hatch It Productions in June 2015 at Trafalgar Studios in London with the following cast:

HUGH	Adam Riches
GEMMA	Hatty Preston
LINDA	Hannah Stokely
WALTER	James Woolley
KRISTON	Tosin Cole
CHRISSIE	Charlie Cameron
EVELYN	Ben Starr

The play was directed by John Schwab
Production Design by Mike Lees
Lighting Design by Catherine Webb
Wardrobe Design by Jo Lewis
Sound Design by Jonathan Cook
Stage Management by Brian Perkins

To All Actors Everywhere

CHARACTERS

In order of speaking:

CHRISSIE THE STAGE MANAGER. 20–25. She is hard working, loyal and willing to do anything to help the show go on.

HUGH LEAD ACTOR 40–45. He has never found the fame, fortune and acclaim which he believes he has deserved and is now painfully vain, insecure and very needy.

GEMMA LEAD ACTRESS 25–30. She is a dedicated and accomplished actress who masks her lack of confidence by pretending to be younger and more foolish than she really is.

EVELYN DIRECTOR 25–55. The spoiled son of accomplished parents whom he has always tried and failed to live up to. He signally lacks any of the artistic or personal qualities required to direct a play.

LINDA ACTRESS 50–55. A competent and clever performer. She is independently wealthy and so doesn't need to work. Acting is, therefore, something of a hobby for her.

WALTER ACTOR – 65+. A jobbing character actor, nearing the end of a long, varied but not terribly illustrious career. But whilst he struggles with remembering his lines, he does have an inexhaustible fund of anecdotes and an inexcusable desire to tell them.

KRISTON STAR ACTOR 20–25. A young, hip, Afro-American who is brought in at great expense to save the day. He is open and willing to please but smart enough not to allow himself to be exploited.

The action takes place in a rehearsal room and then on the stage.

TIME: The present

ACT I

Rehearsal

HUGH *and* GEMMA *are lounging in the stalls, reading their scripts.* CHRISSIE *is taping up the floor.*

Apart from four chairs which have been pushed together to make a sofa, the stage is bare.

Slowly GEMMA, HUGH *and* CHRISSIE *get themselves ready to start.*

HUGH *waits quietly at the back of the stage for his cue.*

GEMMA *stands passively at the front of the stage, looking blankly out at the audience, ready to start.*

CHRISSIE, *reads from a copy of the script...*

CHRISSIE The Dark Heart of Art by Hildred McCann. Scene one. We are in the plush opulence of Linda and Michael's sumptuous loft apartment. It drips with wealth and taste. Original works of stunning art adorn the antiseptic white of the walls, garishly tattooing them with vivid splashes of daring colour and form. There is a marble indoor fountain bubbling in one corner and the couple's pet monkey scampers around the room with innocent chattering abandon. Linda, a woman, is standing in front of a full-length shabby chic mirror, reminiscent of the Egyptian glass in which Darley first catches sight of Justine in volume one of Laurence Durrell's Alexandria Quartet. As the lights come up, she is applying her makeup.

On cue, GEMMA *starts miming making up her face in a mirror.*

Her strong, confident hands move with precision and grace across the flawless features of her chiselled beauty and, beneath their practised and expert menstruation… *ministration,* the face of a proud but strangely vulnerable woman emerges.

GEMMA *does her best to look proud but strangely vulnerable.*

From upstairs we hear the front door shut and then Michael descends the ornate spiral staircase like a confident swan landing on his favourite millpond.

HUGH *has stood up and walked onto the stage and started miming walking down a spiral staircase. They both read from their scripts.*

HUGH "Linda."

GEMMA "Michael!"

She turns and rushes over to him, almost colliding with the four chairs. There is then a slightly over-long pause whilst he stops spiralling. She then embraces him, rather more tightly than necessary.

"You're home."

HUGH "Yes. Home. Back where I started out this morning."

He goes and sits on the chairs but she remains standing.

GEMMA "How was your day?"

Because she is still standing, he stands up again.

HUGH "My day?"

She sits on the chairs and so he follows suit and sits.

GEMMA "Yes. How was your day, teaching at that school you teach at?"

HUGH "My day was a day, a day like any other day. A day like *every* other day. It broke like an egg and smeared itself across the plate of the morning. The clock ticks on and the world races by, past me, busy and occupied – preoccupied and self-obsessed. Passing me by day by day by bye-bye day. And today? Today was just another day. Gone. Past. Another day older but none the wiser."

He pauses. Has he finished the speech? Finally GEMMA *comes in with her line.*

GEMMA "Keep strong my..."

No, he hadn't finished.

HUGH "Just another day closer to the end."

GEMMA Sorry. "Keep strong, my darling."

HUGH "Strong? For what? For who?"

He frowns as he notices there is an "m" missing. He adds it in with a pencil. This confuses GEMMA.

...m."

LINDA "For us. For me...m. You know I think you're a genius."

HUGH "Do you?"

GEMMA "Yes. Isn't that enough?"

CHRISSIE He goes to speak but there are no words and he turns away from her.

HUGH *turns away. They both have to wait, consciously, until the end of the next, interminable stage direction.*

All of the emotion and wellspring of desire flap frantically in his breast like a seagull trapped in a picnic basket. How can a man so full and vibrant feel so crushed and empty?

He can't go on and yet he will. He sighs the soft sigh of a man riding a carousel of disappointment...

HUGH *sighs.*

HUGH No, wait.

He sighs again.

Yes, that's the one.

CHRISSIE ...and wheels back to face the woman who has so faithfully and lovingly remained on his team at his side in his corner.

HUGH *turns back to* **GEMMA** *but she stands up and starts aimlessly (and directionless-ly) wandering the stage.*

HUGH "But do you really, Linda? I know you say you do but do you *really* know what it's like?"

Because she is not with him on the sofa he has to get up and start following her around the stage.

"Having to teach other people's art when all you want to do is create your own. Do you know what that does to your heart? To your soul?"

CHRISSIE He crumples to the sofa like a spent tissue as his wife gently cradles him to her like a distressed orphan. Or a puppy.

During this **HUGH** *and* **GEMMA** *have had to rush to the four chairs and act out the stage direction.*

GEMMA "There, there, darling boy. I know it's hard for you at the moment but you have to work to support us, just until the world recognises you and your work."

HUGH "I know that. But when, Linda? When?"

EVELYN *calls out from the auditorium.*

EVELYN And... Stop!

HUGH *and* GEMMA *immediately break character and look out front as their director makes his way up to the stage.*

I think that's a good place to take a break. Well done. First time through on its feet. Talking of which, Gemma, just be a bit careful where you wander...

GEMMA You didn't like the movement? I thought it was a bit static without moving.

EVELYN No, no, I liked it. It was good. It was...kinetic and gave an energy to the scene but a couple of times you walked through the ornamental fountain. So...

HUGH Is there going to be an actual, real, practical fountain?

EVELYN It's in the script. Also, guys, remember, don't tread on the monkey.

CHRISSIE About that, Evelyn...

EVELYN Hmm?

CHRISSIE I don't know that we'll be able to have a real...live monkey.

EVELYN It's in the script.

CHRISSIE I know but...

HUGH Why do they have a monkey?

GEMMA It's a pet.

EVELYN It's in the script.

HUGH Why can't they have a cat?

GEMMA Because they have a monkey. Because he's an artist. Because it's...you know...

HUGH No. I don't know.

GEMMA It's dramatic. It's unexpected.

EVELYN And in the script.

CHRISSIE But I think there's regulations and stuff. We'll need a...monkey licence.

EVELYN So?

CHRISSIE And we'll need to find a monkey.

HUGH I think we could lose the monkey.

GEMMA I like the monkey.

EVELYN We can't lose the monkey. The monkey is in the script.

HUGH Only at the beginning.

EVELYN We are *not* losing the monkey. Chrissie...

CHRISSIE Yes, Evelyn?

EVELYN Get a monkey licence and get a monkey?

> CHRISSIE *nods and pulls out her phone.*

CHRISSIE Right.

EVELYN Also, remember, I want you to really play those moments.

CHRISSIE What kind of monkey? Big monkey? Small monkey?

GEMMA Pet monkey.

EVELYN Get me a few monkeys. I'll audition them.

CHRISSIE Right.

EVELYN Choices.

CHRISSIE Choices. Right.

> *She gets out her phone and starts Googling.*

Okay Google.

EVELYN Good. Now...

HUGH Evelyn...

EVELYN Hugh...

HUGH While we're stopped...

CHRISSIE *talks to her phone.*

CHRISSIE "Give me monkey choices".

EVELYN Yes...

HUGH I was just wondering...

EVELYN Wondering?

HUGH Yes. About the set. The apartment. With the fountain, and the artwork and stairs...

GEMMA And the monkey.

HUGH And the monkey, yes...

GEMMA I love it. It's so...bold and striking and...you know.

HUGH Yes, I know...

EVELYN It's *so* Hildred-esque.

HUGH Yes, but...

GEMMA It's going to make such an impression on the audience.

HUGH Stop.

EVELYN Problem, Hugh?

HUGH Yes. Is it in character?

EVELYN Character? Is the set in character?

HUGH Yes. He's a teacher, right.

GEMMA Only until he's discovered as an artist. He's only working as a teacher because he has to.

EVELYN Like it says in the script.

HUGH Yes, I know that. But...

EVELYN But?

HUGH Well, how much do teachers earn?

EVELYN I really have no idea. Chrissie?

CHRISSIE I'm not sure. But I don't think it's very much. I think they're a bit like nurses.

HUGH Yes. That's what I thought.

GEMMA But he's not a nurse, is he? He's an artist.

HUGH Who has to work as a teacher. So he's not going to be rich, is he. I mean, rich enough to have a real fountain and a pet monkey.

EVELYN For the last time, people, we're not losing the monkey.

GEMMA Well, maybe she works. Does something in a bank. They earn buckets of money.

HUGH But it doesn't say in the script.

EVELYN Not at the moment. In this draft. But it's a good draft and it's a good point, Hugh.

GEMMA A good point for a good draft.

EVELYN Thank you, Gemma. Hugh. This is what this process is all about. It's a new play. It's a brand new Hildred. An exciting journey. We are giving birth in an almost literal sense to the writer's words and these are all the things that you'll be able to discuss when Hildred comes in.

GEMMA When is Hildred coming in?

EVELYN Chrissie?

CHRISSIE I haven't heard yet from him.

EVELYN I've asked for a little time to ourselves, to bond together as a company, to get the play on its feet – stop splashing through the fountain...

GEMMA Squashing the monkey.

EVELYN Exactly. And Hildred's been very understanding and supportive of that.

HUGH Yes. But he will be coming to rehearsals.

EVELYN Of course. And you will have the chance to discuss all these little points then. And, do you know something, Hugh, I know the play, *our* play will grow and evolve as we all go along our path together.

GEMMA Well said, Evelyn.

EVELYN Thank you, Gemma.

GEMMA That was beautifully put.

EVELYN I meant it all.

GEMMA No, it was really heartfelt and wise and...you know. Really.

CHRISSIE There's a petting zoo near Rotherham that hires out monkeys.

EVELYN Brilliant. There you see. Well done, Chrissie.

CHRISSIE I'll call them.

Dialling, she rushes out.

EVELYN And we will carry on with the scene.

HUGH Yes. But...

EVELYN But?

HUGH About my entrance down the spiral staircase.

EVELYN Like a swan landing on a favourite millpond.

GEMMA Wonderful imagery.

HUGH Yes, I'm working on the swan.

He makes a ludicrous swan gesture.

I think I'm almost there on that. It's just...

EVELYN Just?

HUGH This is a loft apartment, right?

EVELYN Right.

HUGH And I'm coming home from work.

GEMMA As a teacher and an artist.

EVELYN Yes.

HUGH Down the stairs...

EVELYN So?

HUGH So have I been on the roof?

EVELYN Stop!

He takes a deep breath and then walks out shouting as he goes.

Chrissie! We're going to take a little break now.

GEMMA Shall we go through the script?

There is a scene change.

It is the next day and all the company has been called. **LINDA** *(the actress who will be playing Samantha) and* **WALTER** *(the actor who will be playing Joe) enter and join* **GEMMA** *and* **HUGH**. *They are carrying chairs, which they plonk themselves down on. As she comes on,* **LINDA** *brandishes her script.*

LINDA It's changed.

HUGH Changed?

LINDA The script.

HUGH What?

LINDA Didn't you get the rewrite?

HUGH When?

LINDA Last night. Don't you check your emails, Hugh.

GEMMA Exciting. I love getting rewrites. Don't you, Linda?

WALTER I never "check my emails".

GEMMA Don't you, Walter?

WALTER I'm afraid I'm all rather stupid with technology.

HUGH So what's changed?

WALTER I like it when things come in the post.

HUGH Am I still a teacher?

LINDA Yes. But you're not really an artist any more.

HUGH What?

WALTER But they never do.

GEMMA I find it exhilarating. And this is apparently what Hildred does. The piece changes and grows every day.

HUGH But the entire play is about me being discovered as an artist.

LINDA It was.

HUGH What?

LINDA It's changed.

GEMMA So exciting.

HUGH Has my speech gone?

> HUGH *grabs* LINDA's *script and starts scanning through it.*

LINDA 'Fraid so.

GEMMA It's stimulating.

HUGH Bollocks. I'd just learnt it.

WALTER I never learn anything too quickly.

> GEMMA *is now a bit concerned.*

GEMMA Ooh, has my part changed?

WALTER Mind you, I also have trouble learning things slowly too.

HUGH There's whole scenes of mine gone!

LINDA It seems to be more about Linda now.

GEMMA Really? How exciting for you.

LINDA No, Gemma luv, it's not more about me, Linda. It's more about you, Linda.

GEMMA Really? Oh, that's nice.

HUGH *is still scanning the script.*

HUGH There's lots of stage directions.

LINDA Yes. Hildred likes directions, doesn't he.

HUGH I have to pick up my coat "in my tortured hands like I'm strangling a childhood kitten".

GEMMA Gosh. That's...powerful.

HUGH But I don't get to say much.

WALTER I've not been cut down, have I?

LINDA No.

WALTER Pity.

LINDA But you're not Michael's dad anymore.

WALTER Then who am I?

LINDA Linda's dad.

GEMMA Me, Linda?

WALTER I'm not too sure about that.

HUGH Quite right, Walter. It's a whole different character you've been given.

WALTER No, I'll do the same performance I always do, I just hope the words aren't too different.

LINDA But I didn't think you'd learnt it, yet.

WALTER No, I haven't. But some bits were starting to feel sort of...familiar.

HUGH Well, I'm not happy with this.

WALTER Like an old coat.

HUGH I was contracted to play a role, a character, and I've already started the process of creation.

GEMMA But this is what happens with new writing, Hughie. It's alive and growing and...

HUGH And it's Hugh. I have been inhabiting Michael, my Michael and I can't just cast him off like an old coat.

GEMMA But he's not *your* Michael, is he?

HUGH Well, he's not any more.

GEMMA He's the writer's Michael. He's Hildred's Michael.

HUGH Well, frankly, I think Hildred's taking the Michael.

LINDA Oh, that's very good. Was that meant to be a joke?

HUGH No, Linda, it wasn't. I don't think the writer has the right to change the play once rehearsals have started.

LINDA "The writer has the write"?

HUGH You know what I mean. I'm not happy and I'm going to talk to Evelyn about it.

He throws his script in the air and EVELYN *enters through the shower of pages.*

EVELYN Good morning troops!

HUGH Hello.

EVELYN Hughie. Ready for another bright new day on our continuing voyage of exploration and discovery.

GEMMA Rather.

LINDA Hughie's not happy.

EVELYN Really? Morning Walter. You're looking well.

WALTER Am I?

HUGH Actually, I'm not happy.

EVELYN I know that, Hugh. And it's wonderfully in character of you. And how's my Linda this morning?

GEMMA Me, Linda?

EVELYN No, you Gemma, she Linda.

LINDA I'm fine thanks, Evelyn.

GEMMA And so am I.

EVELYN And are you happy?

GEMMA I'm happy, excited and...

EVELYN There, you see, Hugh, Gemma's happy.

GEMMA And so's Linda.

LINDA Am I?

HUGH Well, she would be, wouldn't she. It's not her part that's getting cut to ribbons.

EVELYN Hugh. No one's part is getting cut to ribbons.

LINDA *(to* HUGH*)* Except yours.

HUGH Thank you, Linda.

WALTER If you want to cut my bits down, I don't mind.

EVELYN Thank you Walter but it's not a question...

HUGH There. Why don't you cut Walter's part? He doesn't mind.

EVELYN It's not a question of cutting anyone's part.

HUGH He hasn't even learnt it yet.

WALTER It's becoming familiar.

EVELYN The play is changing.

WALTER But slowly.

GEMMA It's *evolving*.

EVELYN Exactly, Gemma. Well said.

WALTER Like an old coat.

GEMMA Your words, Evelyn.

EVELYN Then it was even better said.

HUGH I learnt my scene one speech.

WALTER That was a bit quick off the mark, Hugh old lad.

LINDA Think you're going to have unlearn it, aren't you.

WALTER I find I can do that bit okay these days.

HUGH Yes, *Thank You* Linda!

GEMMA Me Linda?

LINDA I'm just saying.

WALTER Mind you, it wasn't always the way. I've still got bits of Mercutio stuck in there from 1986.

EVELYN Stop!!!

Pause – they all stop.

Can we just start?

HUGH I know what you were just saying and it's not very helpful.

LINDA But it's true.

EVELYN Where's Chrissie?

WALTER "Oh, then I see Queen Mab hath been with you. She is the fairies's midwife and she comes in shape no bigger than an agate stone on the forefingers of an alderman."

LINDA Rotherham.

EVELYN What the hell is she doing in Rotherham?

LINDA Search me.

WALTER "Drawn with a team of little atomies over men's noses as they lie asleep.."

EVELYN Did she leave the new scripts?

HUGH Why don't we just stick to the old ones?

GEMMA This is SO exciting.

WALTER "Her chariot is an empty hazelnut, made by the joiner squirrel or old grub, time out o'mind the fairies' coach maker."

HUGH What are you rattling on about, Walter?

EVELYN Can we *please* start?

WALTER It's still in there, see. Word perfect after all these years.

LINDA I think she wanted us to print out our own copies.

WALTER Mind you, I cocked up on opening night.

EVELYN Oh, Christ!

HUGH Walter...?

WALTER Romeo and Juliet in Guildford.

LINDA It's what she said in the email.

HUGH I thought it was in Verona.

GEMMA Fresh, new and...words, waiting for us every day.

LINDA Didn't you get it?

WALTER Smashing production.

EVELYN So we don't have the new script?

LINDA I've got mine.

GEMMA We won't know what we're doing from day to day.

WALTER I wish we were doing that play.

EVELYN Right, well, we're just going to have to start.

HUGH I wish we were still doing the play we were doing yesterday.

LINDA I'm ready when you are, Evelyn.

GEMMA It's a real adventure.

HUGH I'm not happy.

WALTER So what are we doing?

EVELYN Can we please *start*?

LINDA Where are we going from?

HUGH When's the writer going to come in?

GEMMA Oh! I haven't got a script?

WALTER It's just I'm no good with emails and whatnot.

GEMMA Has anyone got a script for me?

HUGH I think we should have a meeting with him.

LINDA Are we going to start?

EVELYN STOP!!!

Everyone stops.

Let's just get this over with, shall we? Scene four. Hugh, you're there, Gemma over there and Linda on the other side. I need to feel the distance...the spaces between you all. Let's go.

They get into position and start the scene – but GEMMA and LINDA have to keep crossing over to pass the script.

LINDA "When did you first realise that your husband was a genius?"

LINDA crosses and passes the script to GEMMA and crosses back.

GEMMA "You think he's a genius?"

GEMMA crosses and passes the script to LINDA and crosses back.

LINDA "You mean you don't?"

LINDA crosses and passes the script to GEMMA and crosses back.

EVELYN Stop!!! What are you doing?

LINDA Only one script.

EVELYN Chrissie!

LINDA Rotherham.

EVELYN Shit.

GEMMA Evelyn. How about we move closer?

EVELYN I want distance.

LINDA How about we move distantly closer.

EVELYN Try it.

> GEMMA *and* LINDA *shuffle a bit closer and the scene continues.*

GEMMA "I know he's the man I married. My life partner. My significant other."

LINDA "And this precludes him from genius?"

EVELYN Uh huh. That works.

GEMMA "It's certainly not a prerequisite. Although genius is an admirable quality."

LINDA "In a husband or an artist?"

GEMMA "Both. Although there are many who get by as either with none."

LINDA "And therein lies the tragedy."

GEMMA "For art or marriage?"

LINDA "Both."

EVELYN They laugh like cut glass Christmas baubles tinkling down a mountain stream.

> GEMMA *and* LINDA *try out various tinkling laughs.*

LINDA "But..."

GEMMA "Yes?"

LINDA "There is something."

GEMMA "There's always something."

LINDA "Something I wanted to ask."

GEMMA "Me?"

LINDA "Of course you. Who else?"

GEMMA "Ask away."

LINDA "Where does it all come from?"

HUGH Can we stop, please?

EVELYN Problem, Hugh?

HUGH Question, Evelyn. Why is she asking Linda?

GEMMA Me Linda?

HUGH I mean, how the hell is *she* going to know where the inspiration and genius comes from? I mean, I am standing here actually *being* the genius, you know, like, painting a masterpiece and everything, so why is she asking her and not me?

EVELYN Yes. You know, that is a good question.

HUGH So what's the answer?

EVELYN It's in the script. Now, can we get on with the scene?

GEMMA "The inspiration. The art. The genius?"

LINDA Yes. "The inspiration. The art. The genius?"

There is a pause.

GEMMA "The inspiration. The art. The genius?"

LINDA Yes... *Linda...*" The inspiration. The art. The genius." Can *you* tell *me* where does it all come from?

GEMMA "The inspiration...

LINDA "...the art and the genius." Yes. That's my line.

GEMMA Is it? Sorry. It's just it's highlighted and...

LINDA That's because it's my script. Look...

She shows her the front page.

... "Linda".

GEMMA I thought I was Linda.

LINDA No, you're Gemma.

EVELYN Oh, for Christ's sake!

GEMMA Oh yes. Sorry. Sorry, Evelyn, my mistake everybody. Me Gemma, you Linda.

LINDA No, Gemma, you Linda, me Samantha, he Michael but this, my script.

EVELYN Can we *please* get on?

GEMMA Go back?

HUGH To my line?

LINDA God! Not that far. Here...

She points to a place in the script for **GEMMA**.

"Where does it all come from?"

GEMMA "What?"

LINDA "The inspiration. The art. The genius?"

GEMMA "When I was a child, seven years old, I yearned for a pot. To have something beautiful, of my own, to love and care for, to nurture and watch grow..." Oh, it was *pet*! "I told my parents and they, lovingly misguided, offered me a kitten. Then a puppy, then a rabbit, a goldfish, even some bizarre creature they called a German...*gerbil*, all of which I swiftly and shudderingly rejected. How could I explain? I lacked the language...the *art* to tell them what it was I wanted. Until, one sunlit, magical afternoon when from out of the clear blue sky a butterfly fluttered by and landed on my hand. It was so beautiful. I couldn't speak. But I didn't need to speak. The painful beauty of this creature had become my language and my art. I rushed it inside, to my room and put it in a jar. Where it died."

EVELYN That was wonderful, Gemma.

HUGH Didn't really answer the question though, did it.

LINDA "I think I understand."

HUGH I'm glad someone does.

GEMMA "Yes. You see, art is like a butterfly. If you put it in a jar it dies."

There is a pause. Finally...

LINDA Hugh?

HUGH What?

LINDA It's your line.

HUGH Oh. I actually get a line do I?

He is handed the script. He studies it then nods.

It's in.

He hands the script back, composes himself and then...

"Ssssh."

He looks up. LINDA, GEMMA *and* EVELYN *are all looking at him critically.*

What?

EVELYN That's not how you're thinking of doing it, is it?

HUGH Yes. I think so. Probably. Why?

They all look at him doubtfully.

What?

GEMMA Well...

LINDA It's one way, I suppose.

GEMMA Every choice is valid.

LINDA Yes. Everything. Except that one maybe.

EVELYN We can work on it.

HUGH Work on it?

EVELYN Yes. We can work on the line with you.

HUGH Line? What do you mean "line"? It's a noise. An exhalation. It's not so much a line as a fart.

EVELYN But it's frightfully important.

LINDA Absolutely it is. After all Hugh, it's one of the very few times we hear anything from you now.

GEMMA Your fart is crucial.

EVELYN Well put, Gemma.

HUGH Right! That's it. I've had enough of this.

He makes as if to leave but **EVELYN** *quickly heads him off.*

EVELYN Hugh. I'm sensing you're struggling.

HUGH No, Evelyn, I'm not struggling. I'm walking. Out.

EVELYN You can't do that.

GEMMA That's right. We'd miss you.

LINDA A bit.

HUGH When I agreed to do this, I clearly understood that I was playing the *lead role* in a new play. Not providing crucial background flatulence.

LINDA But you do it so well.

GEMMA That's right, Hughie.

EVELYN And it's *so* much more than that. Hugh, in so many ways, this scene, this whole play is all about you.

LINDA Except you don't say anything.

EVELYN No. But then I really do believe that your character, Michael, Hugh, *doesn't need to say anything* to command the scene. *That* is how strong this part is.

HUGH But in the first draft I had speeches and dialogue and...

EVELYN And now...now, what the writer is doing is strengthening your central role in the piece by letting the other characters do all that for you, leaving you free to concentrate on your inner performance.

HUGH *likes the sound of this.*

HUGH "Inner" performance.

EVELYN Absolutely. Because it's that interior world, the private core of the artist that I honestly believe this play is really exploring.

HUGH Really?

EVELYN Absolutely. This is what the writer is reaching for. And this is why he needs... I need...the play needs a remarkable... exceptional actor. A *re*-actor

GEMMA It's SO exciting.

EVELYN And I thought we had found that re-actor.

LINDA Really?

EVELYN But, you know something, Hughie, that's always been my weakness. Seeing greatness in others which maybe is too much to expect.

HUGH Well, I wouldn't be too hasty.

EVELYN It's not your fault, it's mine. It's not your failing, it's me. It's always me. I see an actor, a player, a *talent*, like you and I ask too much.

HUGH Don't be too hard on yourself, Evelyn.

EVELYN Time after time. I ask actors to take me to places that I could never dare go alone.

HUGH Hey. It's what we do, you know.

EVELYN No, Hugh. I can't make you do this. Not for me. Because if the road is too hard for you to travel...

HUGH I wouldn't say that...

EVELYN ...if your courage is failing you, then believe me, I would be the last to cast the first stone and condemn you.

HUGH Evelyn...

EVELYN I am a monster and must be stopped... Walk! I respect your decision.

LINDA I've got a friend who does a lot of commercials who could step in.

EVELYN Is he a name?

LINDA More of a voice. He does the Meerkat.

GEMMA Oooh. Can he get me a baby Oleg?

HUGH Now, stop.

EVELYN You still here, Hugh?

HUGH Of course I am, Evelyn. Look, I'm not one to run away from a challenge. Even one as tough as this.

EVELYN *turns back to face him.*

EVELYN I don't know, Hugh. I don't know that I can do this to you. I don't know it's *fair.* Linda, is your Meerkat friend busy?

LINDA I can check.

HUGH No. Stop. Stop. Evelyn, no matter how tough the path... I'll walk it with you. Mate.

There is a bromantic moment and then HUGH *and*
EVELYN *embrace.* GEMMA *is moved...*

GEMMA Oh!

LINDA *isn't...*

LINDA God!

EVELYN Right! Now, let's get back to it. And remember Hughie...

HUGH Yes, Evie...lyn.

EVELYN We're in this together. Right?

HUGH Right!

EVELYN Shoulder to shoulder. Arm in arm. Comrades to the
end. Now...go do as you're told.

HUGH Where do you want me?

EVELYN Right where you belong. At the easel. Centre stage.

HUGH Now, if you put it like that.

EVELYN I do.

HUGH Understood.

Full of enthusiasm, he takes up his position again as
WALTER *wanders in. He has been dozing somewhere*
off stage.

WALTER Am I in this bit yet?

HUGH Quick question, skipper.

LINDA Not yet, Walter.

EVELYN Fire away.

HUGH What am I actually doing in this scene?

EVELYN It's all here in the script.

He takes the script from LINDA *thumbs through it and*
then reads.

WALTER Good. Give me a shout if you get to me, will you, love.

He starts to leave.

EVELYN "And as the scene ends and the light flutters and dies like a mayfly in a honeypot, the pinkly naked Linda picks up her abandoned clothing from the floor..."

Hearing this, **WALTER** *stops.*

GEMMA What?

EVELYN "...where she has scattered them like the wanton peelings of her sexual fruit."

GEMMA Is that *her,* Linda?

LINDA No, that's *you,* Gemma.

GEMMA Pinkly naked sexual fruit?

WALTER Actually, I think I'll stay and watch for a bit.

EVELYN And you, Hugh, Michael, "finish the painting in a thundering spurt of inspiration."

GEMMA Er... Evelyn?

HUGH Now that does sound powerful.

EVELYN It is. It's a brand new direction for the play.

GEMMA What exactly has been happening in this scene?

WALTER Am I in it, at all?

EVELYN It's terribly thrilling.

GEMMA Yes, but...how do I end up all pinkly naked?

LINDA I think you're his muse. Or something.

EVELYN Exactly.

GEMMA Do I have to get nuddy?

WALTER Does she?

EVELYN It's in the script.

HUGH So what exactly am I painting?

GEMMA I mean this wasn't agreed when I took the part.

EVELYN *consults the script.*

EVELYN Here we are...

WALTER I got my kit off in Leatherhead in 1976.

EVELYN "All through Linda's lascivious display..."

LINDA That's you, Linda.

WALTER It was during a performance of Equus.

EVELYN "...Michael has been lost in a maelstrom of brilliance..."

HUGH Yes!

WALTER I was only an usher at the time, but it got me noticed.

EVELYN "...and in front of our very eyes, he has painted the bare naked form of his exposed wife's cerise volvo..."

GEMMA I might have to talk to my agent about this.

EVELYN "...as the gloriously beautiful butterfly of her innocent childhood."

LINDA That's a hell of an image.

HUGH It's brilliant, Evelyn.

EVELYN I know.

HUGH There's just one thing.

EVELYN What's that?

HUGH I can't actually paint butterflies.

EVELYN Stop!!!

There is a scene change.

It is the start of another day of rehearsal.

HUGH *stands alone doing tai-chi and vocal warm up exercises.*

WALTER *is studying the* Guardian *crossword.*

GEMMA *and* LINDA *are sharing weird tea from a thermos.*

GEMMA Do you think Hugh's...

LINDA What?

GEMMA You know. "Alright"?

LINDA You mean mentally?

GEMMA Yes. Because...you know... I think he might be...

LINDA A dickhead?

GEMMA ...tense.

LINDA Ah. He's "tense" is he?

GEMMA I think so.

LINDA Gemma, has he asked you to give him a massage?

GEMMA Yes.

LINDA At his flat?

GEMMA Yes. He said we could...

LINDA Go over the play together?

GEMMA Yes. Has he asked you too?

LINDA Not for years he hasn't. He didn't mention your pink nakedness by any chance?

GEMMA Yes. But apparently, thank God, my vulva has been cut.

EVELYN *flies onto the stage holding scripts which he starts to hand around.*

EVELYN Rewrites!

They all fling their old scripts in the air.

HUGH Another one?

WALTER I haven't learnt the last two.

LINDA He does know that we're due to open in less than a week, doesn't he?

EVELYN Of course he knows it. And that's why he is so anxious to get the play as perfect as it can be before then. Listen. Everyone. This is how it is with Hildred. With new writing. Remember? We're all family. All equal partners, finding our way, together, along a fresh...sometimes rocky, uncharted path.

GEMMA You're right, Evelyn. But...

EVELYN There are dangers along the path. There may be sharks...

LINDA Not on a path there wouldn't be.

EVELYN But it's all about discussion and collaboration and...

HUGH So what's changed this time?

EVELYN If you lot would all shut up, I'll tell you!

WALTER I haven't been cut out of the play, have I?

EVELYN No, of course not.

WALTER Pity. Because they'd have to pay me off.

GEMMA I don't have to strip off, do I?

EVELYN No, Gemma, relax.

WALTER I got written out in the third draft by Trevor Griffiths once.

EVELYN Hildred has taken your character in a whole new direction.

WALTER Bastard.

EVELYN In fact, he's taken the entire play in a new and, I have to say, surprising way. It's still a challenging examination of how human relationships are shaped by art...

LINDA So *that's* what it is, is it.

WALTER But I got onto Equity and they had to pay me for the whole run.

EVELYN But it has become so much more daring and shocking.

LINDA It's a shocking play.

EVELYN Absolutely it is.

WALTER Unfortunately it only ran for six performances.

HUGH So what has actually changed?

EVELYN Well, first off, the set has been totally re-imagined.

> CHRISSIE *enters. She has been driving all night and is carrying a large animal cage (presumably containing a monkey).* KRISTON *follows her on.*

CHRISSIE Sorry I'm late, everyone.

EVELYN There's no more fountain, the spiral staircase has gone and we've lost that monkey.

> CHRISSIE *reacts. She turns and leaves with the animal cage.*

But we've now got Kriston.

> *He gestures towards* KRISTON, *who has been hanging back, unsure when to announce himself.*

Who's joining us as an *actor*. Not a monkey, obviously.

GEMMA Hello.

LINDA Hi.

HUGH Welcome aboard.

WALTER You're not replacing me, are you?

KRISTON I don't think so.

EVELYN Of course he's not.

HUGH Stop! Stop. Who is he playing?

The scene changes.

We are back in rehearsal with **CHRISSIE** *reading the stage directions.*

CHRISSIE Doctor DJ Professor Snizzle… Yes, that's what it says, "Snizzle", multi-millionaire gangster rap singer and art collector, explodes into the room, silently dripping with bling and menace. He radiates danger like a dangerous radiator and moves like a cobra on springs.

KRISTON *reads from his script.*

KRISTON "Yo. Word up y'all, know what I'm saying. I be here now and I'm bringing it, yo know what I mean. I mean, yo know, representing the brothers and sisters in the struggle, yo know what I mean. 'Cause it's what we all live and it's where I'm all from, yo know what I'm saying, I'm from the ghettos and the projects. The Everyday Struggle. I been in them predicaments, I know them streets, yo know what I'm saying. It's what made me, yo know what I'm saying. I'm saying if I'm good, it's what made me good. And if I'm bad, then it's what made me bad. Yo know what I'm saying. I am what yo made me, man. But I got paid, yo know what I'm saying. I'm saying I got mine. I blowed up and got paid and now I'm bringing it, with love, yo know what I'm saying. I got so much love and respect that yo can't disrespect that love that I'm bringing, yo know what I'm saying, because I'm down and keeping it real. I'm keeping it real amongst all the haters and the suck-ass fakers that don't do shit, yo know what I'm saying? Well, I ain't clowning, yo know what I'm saying, I'm saying I got mine and I'm here to make it right and if I be doing my business and yo be doing your business, yo know what I'm saying, then we be in business, dog. Yo know what I'm saying."

HUGH, GEMMA, LINDA *and* **WALTER** *have been looking at him dumbfounded.*

HUGH Can we stop there, please? I'm sorry, I haven't got a clue what he's saying.

CHRISSIE It's what's in the script.

KRISTON I think it's how white English people think black Americans speak.

GEMMA Yes, that's what I thought it was. It was very good.

KRISTON I do a lot of parts like this.

WALTER I was quite enjoying it.

HUGH You understood it?

WALTER No. But it sounded quite fun.

GEMMA Oh yes, Kriston, I thought you did it really well...

KRISTON Thank you.

HUGH Yes, you were very good. But what did it *mean*?

KRISTON I dunno. I just got here.

WALTER I haven't understood anything that's gone on in this play since I first read it.

> **EVELYN** *comes in and joins them.*

EVELYN Why have we stopped, Chrissie?

CHRISSIE I think everyone needs a bit of direction.

HUGH Or translation.

WALTER Mind you, I did a Stoppard in Reading in 1982 and never had a clue what it was about.

LINDA I think we're all a little bit lost, Evelyn.

HUGH It's this new character who's just come in.

EVELYN Something wrong with Kriston?

GEMMA No, he was marvellous.

LINDA Really strong.

CHRISSIE Word perfect.

WALTER Ended up getting nominated for an award for it from the Reading Advertiser.

HUGH Only we couldn't help wondering...

EVELYN Yes Hugh?

HUGH ...how he, sort of, fits in.

WALTER I didn't get it, though. The play or the award.

EVELYN Are you saying you have some sort of problem with Kriston being here, Hugh?

HUGH What?

EVELYN You're saying he doesn't fit in?

HUGH Oh gosh, no! Absolutely not. I don't know what you're suggesting.

EVELYN Who said I was suggesting anything?

LINDA That's right, Hugh. No one's saying anything about you being a racist.

HUGH I'm not!

GEMMA We know you're not.

LINDA If you say you're not.

HUGH Look. Everyone. I'm not a...you know...anything. I'm just, simply asking, what is *this* man doing here? Not this man, particularly, I mean, this actor – *character*! Made up person. You know what I'm saying?

KRISTON What's he saying?

HUGH I'm saying, who are you and what part do you play in my play?

EVERYONE "Your" play?

HUGH Our play. Collaboration and all that. It's just suddenly we have an... *American* wandering into the action and I was just wondering what the hell he's doing here in the middle of this play about an English teacher with a pet monkey...

EVELYN We've lost the monkey, Hugh.

CHRISSIE Yes, about that, Evelyn...

EVELYN Not now, Chrissie.

HUGH Okay, he doesn't have a monkey but he is a genius and he does paint masterpieces and the play is about that and him and now...there's...well...a sort of... I don't know...a... him...appearing out of nowhere and...what's he doing?

KRISTON Yes, I was sort of wondering that myself.

HUGH Thank you, Kriston.

EVELYN Well, Hugh, if you'd read the play...

HUGH I have read the play, Evelyn! I *keep* reading the play but the play *keeps on changing*!

GEMMA Which is terribly exciting and stimulating and...

WALTER Confusing?

GEMMA Yes.

HUGH So?

EVELYN So?

LINDA So maybe it would be good, now we've stopped, if you could just bring us up to speed with what's happening in the play now.

GEMMA So we know where we all are.

HUGH And who we all are.

WALTER And what the hell's meant to be happening.

EVELYN Oh, very well. Look, it's all terribly simple. It's hardly changed at all. You Hugh, are Michael, a struggling teacher...

HUGH I thought I was an artist.

EVELYN Well, you still can be. There's absolutely nothing to stop you being an artist in your spare time. It's just it's not in the script any more.

HUGH What?

EVELYN But you are still married to Linda...

LINDA Please tell me you mean Gemma.

EVELYN ...who is now a self-obsessed neurotic with multiple personality issues.

LINDA You do mean Gemma. And me? Who am I now?

EVELYN Now, Linda, you're still Samantha, only now you're less an intellectual academic art critic and more a lesbian slut tabloid journalist.

GEMMA Now *that's*...you know...edgy.

WALTER Does she get naked, now?

EVELYN No, Walter. But she does tempt Linda, Gemma, with her forbidden fruit and make her question her role as the dutiful wife.

WALTER And am I still her dad?

EVELYN For the moment, yes.

WALTER Good. Because I'm buggered if I'm changing characters now.

HUGH Evelyn.

EVELYN So, now does everyone know who they are?

HUGH Evelyn.

EVELYN And what they're doing?

HUGH Evelyn!

EVELYN Chrissie. You look like you have a question.

CHRISSIE Have we definitely cut the monkey?

EVELYN Yes. Yes. You've seen the script...

CHRISSIE The latest script?

EVELYN Yes! The script, Chrissie. If you *read the script*, you will see that there is no mention of any monkey any more.

CHRISSIE Definitely.

HUGH Evelyn.

EVELYN Why do you keep going on about the bloody monkey?

CHRISSIE Because they won't take it back.

EVELYN What? Who won't take it back?

CHRISSIE The petting zoo in Rotherham. I've hired it for six weeks.

GEMMA Ahh.

EVELYN You paid for it?

CHRISSIE I had to. They wouldn't just let me take her on trial.

GEMMA Her. It's a little girl monkey.

> **GEMMA** *rushes out excitedly to see the monkey.*

LINDA Then you'd better keep her away from Hugh.

EVELYN What about the audition process?

HUGH Evelyn!

EVELYN Do you mind, Hugh. I'm actually in the middle of something here with Chrissie.

LINDA Unless it gives monkey massages, eh Hughie?

EVELYN Can't you get a refund?

HUGH What do you mean?

LINDA You know what I mean.

HUGH I'm no longer an artist? Evelyn.

WALTER A refund on a monkey?

EVELYN I never said you weren't an artist, Hugh.

LINDA Are you never going to grow up!

CHRISSIE I didn't have any choice, Evelyn.

GEMMA *rushes back in, nursing her hand, which has just been bitten by the monkey.*

GEMMA Does she have a name?

EVELYN Art is all about choice, Chrissie.

HUGH You said it wasn't in the script any more that I'm an artist.

CHRISSIE But that's not how it works with monkeys.

KRISTON Sorry folks, but am I missing something here?

CHRISSIE It was take her or leave it.

LINDA I nearly threw away everything for you.

CHRISSIE You told me you wanted a monkey.

HUGH I don't mind it changing. A bit.

LINDA You shit!

CHRISSIE And I got you a monkey.

EVELYN It wasn't for you to decide that I wanted a lady monkey.

WALTER A monkey's five hundred quid.

HUGH This play is the story of an artist!

CHRISSIE For six weeks it's a hell of a lot more than that.

GEMMA What's wrong with a lady monkey?

EVELYN I'm not saying there's anything inherently *wrong* with a lady monkey?

HUGH When I signed up for it, this play was about *me*.

GEMMA Good. Because that would be sexist.

WALTER And a pony, that's twenty five quid.

EVELYN How the hell can you be sexist about a monkey?

HUGH No. No, that's not what I'm saying.

GEMMA I'm just saying that monkeys have got rights too.

EVELYN Stop!!!

Silence. Then...

KRISTON While we've stopped, can someone tell me who I am and what I'm doing in this play?

HUGH Didn't you get the rewrite?

The scene changes.

We are back in rehearsal. CHRISSIE *reads the stage direction.*

CHRISSIE "As DJ Snizzle penetrates their sanctum they fall as silent as a tomb of an unknown soldier."

KRISTON "Yo."

HUGH "Hello. Can I help you?"

KRISTON "Maybe yes yo can, maybe no yo can't, yo know what I'm saying, dog?"

LINDA "You're Doctor DJ Professor Snizzle!"

KRISTON "Word up."

GEMMA "The renowned rap singer and gangster."

KRISTON "Yo, y'all, that be me. The lyrical, physical S N I double Zee. Was happening ladies?"

HUGH "And didn't I read somewhere that you also own one of the largest collections of street art in the world."

KRISTON "The largest, dog. There ain't a bigger collection than the collection I've collected, yo know what I'm saying."

GEMMA "So what are you doing here? What do you want with us?"

KRISTON "The Banksy, fool. I'm here for the Banksy. You know what I'm saying."

CHRISSIE There is a terrible pause of between seven to nine seconds. But just as the tension reaches boiling point and the psychic ice is about to crack, Linda's father, Joe, breaks into the scene like a egg hurled at a cathedral.

WALTER, *his moment finally arrived, rushes in and opens his mouth to deliver his first line.*

EVELYN And I think that's a good place to stop.

HUGH Banksy? What the hell's Banksy got to do with it?

EVELYN It's in the script, Hugh.

LINDA Didn't you get the rewrite?

KRISTON Another one?

CHRISSIE I emailed it last night.

HUGH *starts scanning through his script.* CHRISSIE *starts clearing up and leaves the stage.*

LINDA While we're stopped Evelyn...

EVELYN I thought you were great, Kriston. Really...

LINDA Can we just talk about the new lesbian scene...

EVELYN ...powerful.

LINDA ...between me and Linda.

GEMMA What, me Linda?

GEMMA *starts anxiously scanning through her script.*

KRISTON Thanks, Evelyn. But this line...

WALTER Do you have any notes for me?

KRISTON "Yo, y'all, that be me. The lyrical, physical S N I double Zee."

EVELYN Great.

KRISTON It doesn't naturally scan.

There is the merest pause.

EVELYN Oh, I think it does.

Realising that he doesn't have a single ally in the room,
EVELYN *closes down, stops listening and starts nodding
and making "Hmm, hmm" noises.*

HUGH It's about a Banksy painting now?

LINDA I mean, I'm not a prude or anything...

GEMMA *has found the scene in her script.*

GEMMA Holy shit!

WALTER I mean, if you want me to change anything, you just say.

LINDA ...I just don't know if it's completely artistically justified.

HUGH I thought *I* did the painting.

GEMMA I'm not doing *that*.

HUGH Evelyn...

KRISTON Could I put another "Zee" at the end of the line?

HUGH ...I thought I was the painter.

GEMMA I don't even know what *that* is.

KRISTON "Yo, y'all, that be me. The lyrical, physical S N I
double Zee Zee."

HUGH Evelyn.

KRISTON What do you think, Evelyn?

WALTER Only say quickly before it starts going in. Okay. Evelyn?

LINDA I think we should change it, Evelyn.

GEMMA I'm not happy, Evelyn.

HUGH Evelyn!!!

EVELYN Hmm?

CHRISSIE *rushes in.*

CHRISSIE Stop!!! Everyone.

EVELYN What?

CHRISSIE The monkey's escaped!

There is a scene change.

It is later. The actors and CHRISSIE *are on a break.*

HUGH What the hell is he talking about? "A protest play"? Since when has it been a protest play?

KRISTON It's a protest play?

LINDA According to Evelyn it is now.

HUGH Don't tell me, "it's in the script".

KRISTON What's it protesting about, exactly?

GEMMA Well, it might not be but I think it's gone too far.

HUGH *comes and stands behind her and starts massaging her shoulders.*

HUGH I agree with you Gemma.

LINDA Yes. But I think we need a script meeting not a massage circle.

GEMMA I agree Gemma, Linda. You.

GEMMA *shrugs him off angrily and he retreats...*

HUGH Of course. Tell Hildred we demand to see him, Chrissie.

CHRISSIE That's not really what I do. Sorry. And I've got to take the butterfly costume back and find pink handcuffs and a nine-inch vibrating strap-on.

GEMMA I'm not doing it!

KRISTON Someone's got to talk to the writer.

CHRISSIE I think Evelyn's on the phone to him now.

LINDA It's no good Evelyn talking to him.

KRISTON I don't understand *what* the play is.

HUGH Well, when we started, it was a play about how a struggling painter is discovered to be a genius.

GEMMA Then it became more about how his wife struggled to come to terms with being married to a genius.

LINDA And now, as far as I can tell, it's a protest about how money corrupts artistic vision.

KRISTON Right.

HUGH It's completely out of control.

LINDA And we're meant to open in four days.

WALTER No one writes protest plays any more. Not like they used to.

HUGH And now, for some reason, the "artistic genius" is suddenly bloody Banksy.

GEMMA He is very good.

KRISTON That is sort of topical.

WALTER Back in my day, agitprop theatre, it was everywhere.

HUGH But *I'm* meant to be the painter.

WALTER All those companies like Belt and Braces and...the other one...

HUGH Me.

WALTER ... 24:7.

LINDA 7:84. But you can't paint, Hugh.

HUGH So?

KRISTON I really don't have any idea what I'm doing in this play. My character. What is my character's doing? Hugh's right.

HUGH Thank you, Kriston.

KRISTON Why does this cartoon, gangsta rapper suddenly pop up out of nowhere?

GEMMA Because it's in the script?

LINDA You sound like our director?

HUGH Oh. Suddenly we have a director?

WALTER Sizwe Banzi.

GEMMA Bless you.

HUGH That's news to me.

KRISTON I just don't understand my character.

HUGH At least you've still got a character.

WALTER Now <u>that</u> was a protest play.

LINDA Oh, for God's sake, Hugh! Why does everything always have to be about you and your bloody ego!

HUGH How...dare you! I think I've had just about enough of you Linda.

GEMMA Her Linda?

HUGH And you. The bloody...pair of you. Bloody Lindas. Well, for your information, I actually *have no ego*. It's the reason I became an actor. And whilst I may not be able to paint, at least I can *pretend*!

And with this he stalks out with all the dignity he can muster.

WALTER It was all about the horrors of life under the apartheid in South Africa.

LINDA Sorry?

KRISTON What was?

WALTER Sizwe Banzi is Dead. I did it in Tunbridge Wells in 1981.

GEMMA Did you really?

LINDA Stop, stop, stop. Walter, you were in Sizwe Banzi is Dead?

WALTER I was.

LINDA By Athol Fugard?

WALTER It was a lovely production. Really powerful.

GEMMA It sounds it.

LINDA But it's a two-hander.

WALTER I know.

LINDA There are only two actors in it.

WALTER I know that.

KRISTON Who did you play?

WALTER Buntu. We did it really authentic. Blackface, the lot.

> **HUGH** *is heard offstage.*

HUGH Oh, for Christ's sake!!!

> *He storms in.*

Stop! Everyone. Stop!!!

CHRISSIE Hugh. What's the matter?

> **HUGH** *holds up a damp sweatshirt.*

HUGH That fucking monkey's pissed all over the dressing room.

> **CHRISSIE** *rushes out as* **EVELYN** *enters.*

EVELYN Okay, everyone, I've just been speaking to Hildred...

> *Everyone speaks at once.*

LINDA At last.

WALTER How is he?

KRISTON What did he say?

HUGH Is he coming in?

GEMMA Will he at least agree to cut the fisting?

EVELYN ...'s answerphone.

This is met with groans.

But...but, people, he did text me straight back.

LINDA What good's that?

EVELYN We had a very good, constructive script...texting session.

HUGH Unbelievable!

EVELYN He's taken all your comments and concerns on board.

GEMMA All of them?

EVELYN Every single one of them. He's listened and he agrees.

HUGH Really?

EVELYN He says your comments have inspired him.

WALTER That sounds dangerous.

EVELYN And he's taking the play in an entirely new direction.

WALTER Told you.

LINDA Not again.

EVELYN And he's setting down immediately to do another complete rewrite.

LINDA We only have three days left, Evelyn! Then there's going to be an audience out there, watching all of this.

HUGH It's going to be a disaster.

EVELYN No it isn't.

KRISTON It will be if we don't know what we're doing.

EVELYN But we will know what we're doing.

WALTER I wouldn't count on it.

EVELYN *Most* of us will know what we're doing.

KRISTON Evelyn. Seriously, man, I have *no* idea what I'm doing.

There is a scene change.

We are rehearsing a scene with **KRISTON** *and* **HUGH**.
CHRISSIE *reads directions, the other actors watch on.*

CHRISSIE Lucian, young, rich, arch and beautiful is holding court to an entranced Michael, who is hanging on his every word like a puppy on a teat.

KRISTON "So, Michael, I may call you Michael, mayn't I?"

CHRISSIE He simpers like a virgin on a saucy picnic, and with his blue eyes ablaze with smouldering passion, he gives an insouciant flick of his tousled blond hair.

KRISTON "But I'm sorry, I haven't properly introduced myself. Lucian Tonderei. Enchanté."

HUGH "The art dealer?"

KRISTON "I like to think of myself as a guerrilla bandit, fighting on the fringes of the outré art world."

CHRISSIE He giggles like a shrewd schoolgirl and flaps out a limp hand in Michael's spellbound direction.

KRISTON Can we stop here? For a moment, please?

EVELYN That was really very good, Kriston. I felt there was so much...connection between the two of you there.

HUGH Oh did you?

EVELYN Absolutely.

KRISTON I don't know. It felt kind of gay.

EVELYN *turns to the others.*

EVELYN Let's throw it open. Any thoughts from the floor?

LINDA I think it's "gurr-riya".

EVELYN What is?

LINDA "Gurr-riya".

WALTER I think it's "gur-illa".

EVELYN Surely, it's "*gare*-rilla".

LINDA No, in Spanish, the double L becomes a Y.

WALTER I might well be, but we're not doing it in Spanish, are we.

GEMMA I've always said, gorilly.

EVELYN The stress is on the first syllable. *Gare*.

WALTER No, in English, it's "gur...illa".

LINDA But it's a Spanish word.

WALTER But he's a English character.

KRISTON I thought I was an American.

EVELYN Not any more.

KRISTON What?

EVELYN Chrissie. Can you check this pronunciation for us?

CHRISSIE Right.

> **CHRISSIE** *pulls out her phone and speaks into it.*

> Okay Google. How do you pronounce...guerrilla...

LINDA Gurr-riya!

WALTER Gurr-illa.

> *She checks the phone.*

EVELYN Well?

CHRISSIE It's come up with the definition of "gala". Sorry.

HUGH Stop!!!

> *Everyone stops.*

> Evelyn. Is he gay?

LINDA Problem with gays as well, Hugh?

HUGH No!

KRISTON I'm kind of asking myself the same sort of question here? What is this "connection" that we're about to feel?

EVELYN Well...that's what we're exploring, isn't it?

HUGH *and* **KRISTON** Is it.

EVELYN We're sort of feeling it out?

GEMMA You really don't have a clue, do you Evelyn.

LINDA There's going to be an audience here in forty-three hours!

WALTER It's gur-illa.

KRISTON Evelyn. I wasn't happy with my character before but, you know, this guy—

EVELYN Is brilliant. Kriston, look, I know it's a new direction, but it's what we have all been experiencing on this production. This is why it's so exciting. It's why we love doing new writing.

KRISTON But I really don't know what to do with this guy.

EVELYN You're doing great. Really. Just one thing. Possibly.

KRISTON What?

EVELYN I think you may be playing him too "black".

Beat.

KRISTON Say what?

EVELYN Just trying to help.

KRISTON I don't think I can do this.

He turns to leave. **EVELYN** *stops him.*

EVELYN I know that's how you feel, Kriston. Believe me I do understand. And I want you to know it's not your fault, it's mine. It's not your failing, it's me.

Having got his attention, **EVELYN** *turns away from him.*

I see an actor, a player, a *talent* like you and I ask too much. I ask you to take me to places that I could never dare go alone. I am a monster to expect it. So, go. If the road is too hard for you to travel, I won't cast the first stone and condemn you. Walk! I respect your decision.

KRISTON Thanks Evelyn. I appreciate it, man.

He walks out. There is a pause.

EVELYN Kriston?

GEMMA He's gone, Evelyn.

EVELYN *whirls around.*

EVELYN Bastard! That always works. Chrissie, get after him and get him back in here.

CHRISSIE Right, Evelyn. Er...how?

EVELYN He's a Yank. Tell him he's got a contract and we'll sue!

HUGH Stop!!!

There is a scene change.

Everyone freezes except HUGH and LINDA.

HUGH *is having a meltdown.*

Stop...stop...stop...stop...

LINDA For God's sake Hugh, pull yourself together.

HUGH I can't. I literally can't.

LINDA No, you figuratively can't, you literally won't.

HUGH Do you ever take a day off from being such a smart-arsed cow, sleep with me?

This really pulls her up short.

Please.

LINDA Hugh...

HUGH Just sex.

LINDA No. Hugh...

HUGH Remember Eastbourne?

LINDA I'm married now.

HUGH You were married then.

LINDA We were...young.

HUGH Well, technically, *I* was young.

LINDA I'm trying to help you here, Hugh.

HUGH Sorry. *(Beat)* Sleep with me?

LINDA Can you hear me?

HUGH Sorry.

LINDA I know what you're going through...

HUGH I very much doubt that.

LINDA Hugh. I'm not going to sleep with you. Again. We're all of us going through hell.

HUGH Maybe we all are. But I'm going through it worse.

LINDA Of course you are. Do you know what Winston Churchill said?

HUGH Sleep with me? On the beaches?

LINDA No. He said, "When you're going through hell...keep going." Don't stop.

Beat.

HUGH Well, bully for Winston bloody Churchill. He only had Adolf Hitler and World War Two to worry about. But this? I tell you, Lindy, this *is* Eastbourne all over again. Remember? Schindler's List.

LINDA The Musical. What were we thinking of?

Behind them, very unobtrusively, **CHRISSIE** *has entered and is clearing up the blizzard of paper that litters the stage. She then starts taking up the tape from the floor.*

But Hugh, my darling...remove your hand...thank you...you are a great actor and it's going to be fine.

Beat.

HUGH I'm not your darling.

LINDA I know. You're also not a great actor and it's not going to be fine but I think we're too far in now to quibble, don't you?

GEMMA Stop!!!

HUGH *and* **LINDA** *freeze (and slowly melt from the stage).* **GEMMA** *and* **WALTER** *unfreeze.*

GEMMA *has been trying to learn her latest lines.*

I'm sorry, Walter, but do you think you could just stop doing what you're doing.

WALTER What I'm doing?

GEMMA Yes. It's just I'm trying to concentrate and it's rather... you know.

WALTER What?

GEMMA Irritating. Sorry.

WALTER That's alright. Only...

GEMMA Hmm?

WALTER What exactly was it I was doing?

GEMMA I don't know exactly. You were just...you know...being you.

WALTER Oh.

GEMMA Sorry.

WALTER No, no. I understand. I'll just try stopping being me, then shall I?

GEMMA If you could. Thanks. It's just...you know...all the... stories and the...anecdotes and the...you know... All the time.

WALTER Right.

GEMMA Sorry.

WALTER No, no. I'm sorry. Mea culpa.

Pause.

It's just how I am.

Pause.

You're not the first to comment on it.

Pause.

Derek Jacobi once told me to "Shut my fucking cake hole". 1989, backstage at Chichester, we were doing *The Rivals*, smashing production and...

GEMMA Stop!!!

*She hurls her script in the air and storms out, colliding with **EVELYN** who is coming in looking for **CHRISSIE**. (**WALTER** waits for a convenient moment to slip away).*

EVELYN Chrissie. Everything good?

CHRISSIE No.

EVELYN Good. Everything's set and ready to go?

CHRISSIE Evelyn, nothing is good, nothing is set and nothing is ready to go.

EVELYN Right. Any problems, just let me know.

CHRISSIE Evelyn! Do you really want to know my problems?

EVELYN Er... Figure of speech, really.

CHRISSIE Because I'm not sure exactly *what* my problem is.

EVELYN Excellent.

He makes to leave again but she holds him there.

CHRISSIE Maybe it's that I haven't slept in two days or washed in six.

EVELYN Eurgh.

CHRISSIE Maybe it's that I spend all my time printing scripts that are rewritten before I can distribute them, or buying props which we don't use or hiring costumes for characters who immediately get written out. Or maybe, it's because I had to explain to my boyfriend that we are now babysitting a redundant monkey for the next six weeks.

EVELYN Oh Chrissie, I'm so sorry. I never realised. You have a boyfriend? Really?

CHRISSIE Had. I *had* a boyfriend. He moved out yesterday when he caught the bloody thing wanking into his Play Station.

EVELYN I thought it was a girl monkey.

CHRISSIE So did I! I was wrong! And now, my *latest* problem is this!

She brandishes the script at him.

Have you read it?

EVELYN Yes. It's really evolving and...

CHRISSIE Stop.

He stops.

Suddenly, now, according to the script, I have to make a full-sized, original Banksy art work materialise out of nowhere across the set.

EVELYN It's going to be breathtaking. A real coup de theatre.

CHRISSIE But how is it going to happen?

EVELYN How do you think? Look, it's all in the script.

He thumbs to the page and reads. As he does, **CHRISSIE** *starts mumbling "stop" to herself, building to the last one.*

In the black inkiness, we hear the sound of genius. Spray cans hiss feverishly, like hectic snakes in a mattress, as a Banksy tour de force blossoms in front of our astounded eyes. It smears and spreads across the walls, filling the stage with its bold and audacious...

CHRISSIE Stop!!!

He stops.

How, Evelyn? Just *how* are we going to do that?

Beat.

EVELYN Lighting.

CHRISSIE Lighting?

EVELYN Yes. We...you can use a... Blow Go.

CHRISSIE It's a gobo.

EVELYN One of those, yes. We'll get a gobo.

CHRISSIE Where from? Things like that have to be made. Made by people who make things. And not by people who prance around, talking shit and...and...

EVELYN Stop! Chrissie, I'm sorry. I can see you're upset but I will not have you talking about the actors like that. However, if there's something you want to get off your chest, then, go ahead. You can tell me. Anything. Everything. What you think. Of the play. Of the production. Of me...

CHRISSIE Oh, you don't want to ask me that, Evelyn...

EVELYN No, Chrissie, I do. You are my right hand. And I rely on you to do all those things that I need my right hand to do. I respect your opinion.

CHRISSIE Evelyn...

EVELYN And I want you to be honest. I want... I need to hear it. Straight.

CHRISSIE You're full of shit. Evelyn. And you couldn't direct traffic out of a paper bag.

Beat.

EVELYN Okay. That's your opinion and...

CHRISSIE No that's what the cast is saying. I just think the play is terrible. The actors hate it, they hate each other and they hate you.

EVELYN Do they? Well. That's interesting because...

CHRISSIE I would imagine that most people you work with hate you.

EVELYN You'd "imagine", would you?

CHRISSIE But I don't think you've done much before this...

EVELYN Well, I don't like to blow my own...

CHRISSIE ...because if you had you wouldn't be so useless.

EVELYN Yeah, alright...

CHRISSIE I don't know if it's because you've got a girl's name...

EVELYN Jesus!

CHRISSIE ...but you have no integrity, no insight and absolutely no talent.

EVELYN What the fuck do you know?

He storms out.

CHRISSIE I did say you didn't want to ask me.

EVELYN *returns.*

EVELYN Chrissie? What am I going to do?

CHRISSIE Cancel.

EVELYN I can't. I've got too much invested in this play.

CHRISSIE Evelyn. I know you think it's an important piece of art...

EVELYN No. I've invested in it. If we cancel I could lose my flat. Again. Mum and Dad will be really pissed off. Again. Chrissie, you've got to help me.

CHRISSIE What do you want me to do?

EVELYN Tell me everything's going to be fine and people are going to love it...

CHRISSIE "Everything is going to be fine."

EVELYN And people are going to love it.

CHRISSIE "Everything is going to be fine."

That's the best he's getting and so he gives a thumbs up and claps his hands.

EVELYN Right! Everyone. Full run through, on stage now!

HUGH, GEMMA, LINDA *and* **WALTER** *enter all babbling.*

HUGH Evelyn, this latest draft...

GEMMA How can we be married but he doesn't know...

LINDA What's my motivation to do this bit...

WALTER Can I just ask about this bit?

HUGH Is it meant to say this?

LINDA Is this a misprint?

WALTER Can I go home?

GEMMA Can I just ask...

EVELYN STOP!!! Everyone.

They all fall silent.

Stop. Thank you. We have no time for questions. The time for questions is over. Now is the time...for acting. From the top!

GEMMA Acting stations!

EVELYN Shut up, Gemma. Let's do it. No stopping!

There is a scene change.

A rapid montage of moments from the manic rehearsals for Banksy Ain't Gay.

The actors move into the middle of the stage with their scripts and do their moments as CHRISSIE *sits at the side and reads the stage directions. We start with* GEMMA *and* HUGH.

GEMMA "Yes. Tell me, Michael. Did you have a good day?"

CHRISSIE Michael gives a dry bitter laugh, like a broken promise in an arid well.

HUGH "My day?"

CHRISSIE He picks up his coat from the back of the chair. But what is the point? He puts it down again.

LINDA "I've got some fish. I thought we could have fish tonight. Would you like some fish?"

EVELYN And stop! That was wonderful, Hugh. And Gemma. Inhabit those lives and don't forget to *really* play those directions.

WALTER *steps in with* GEMMA.

GEMMA "So how did you find me, Dad?"

WALTER *hesitates.*

WALTER Ah...yes... Er...did I ask someone?

EVELYN Nearly, Walter. The line is actually...

As EVELYN *reads the line to* WALTER, *the other actors all mime the action of the line.*

"It were the papers. I saw you in the papers. Soon as I saw you, in the papers, I knew, don't ask me how I did, but I did, I just knew it were you."

WALTER Yes! That's it.

EVELYN Keep working on it.

He leaves and **LINDA** *and* **HUGH** *step in with* **GEMMA.** **LINDA** *mimes being outside and shouting through a letter box.*

GEMMA "Who is it?"

CHRISSIE Michael calls out, coiled like a slinky cobra.

HUGH "Who are you?"

SAM "I'm from the press."

LINDA "What do they want?"

MICHAEL "What do you want?"

SAM "I want to talk to you about Banksy."

EVELYN And stop! Everyone. It's getting there. Remember, this is the crucial point of penetration.

GEMMA Oh, do you have to Evelyn?

EVELYN It's in the script, Gemma.

HUGH *and* **LINDA** *step out and* **WALTER** *steps back in with* **GEMMA.**

GEMMA "So, how did you find me Dad?"

WALTER "It were...something to do with the papers..." Wasn't it?

EVELYN Stop!!!

WALTER No, it was. I'm sure it was.

WALTER *steps out and* **HUGH** *and* **LINDA** *step back in with* **GEMMA.**

LINDA "I told you. I want to talk about Banksy."

GEMMA "We don't know anything about him."

LINDA "No one does. That's why it's a story. He's a gwear-iya. Fighting society from behind a legend. Who is he? Or she? Banksy is no one and at the same time, everyone."

HUGH Stop! I'm sorry but you're not really going to say it like that, are you?

LINDA Like what?

HUGH Gwear-iya.

LINDA It's authentic.

HUGH Sounds mental.

EVELYN Stop!!!

> LINDA *and* GEMMA *step out.* HUGH *takes centre stage.*

HUGH "All my life I've waited for this moment. I've always known it would arrive. Fame? It's no big deal. I knew I was extraordinary and the fact I have no real talent for anything wasn't going to stop me being known."

EVELYN Stop! Hugh. You were *born* to play this part.

HUGH You're too kind, Evelyn. But, we also know you're right.

> HUGH *steps out and* GEMMA *steps back in. She does her best to act out the stage directions.*

CHRISSIE The sun comes up on a new day. From outside, the excited sound of an excited crowd of excited people agitates into the still room. Linda enters, frantic like a lost child in a shopping mall. She opens the closed curtains. The crowd roars like an enraged walrus and flashing flashbulbs flash in a cornucopia of brilliance, making her start like a gazelle on a waltzer. In a panic she shuts the curtains and cowers against the wall, clutching at her stomach like it is a sack of precious venom and screaming soundlessly.

> GEMMA *mimes screaming.*

EVELYN Gemma, love. I can't hear you.

GEMMA I'm being soundless.

EVELYN Yes, but you're also meant to be screaming.

GEMMA Am I?

EVELYN It's in the script.

GEMMA Right. So...er... What shall I...?

EVELYN Split the difference?

GEMMA *(confused)* Right.

> **GEMMA** *steps out and* **HUGH** *and* **CHRISSIE** *step in.*
> **CHRISSIE** *is reading on.*

CHRISSIE "But I'm sorry, I haven't properly introduced myself. Lucian Tonderei."

MICHAEL "The art dealer?"

CHRISSIE "I like to think of myself as a guerrilla bandit, fighting on the fringes of the outré art world. And you must be Michael."

MICHAEL "Yes. How did you..."

CHRISSIE "Oh, come now. *Everyone* knows you. The entire the art world...the entire *nation* knows who you are. The man with the masterpiece on his back wall."

EVELYN And stop! It's not bad. Definitely on the way. Shaping up.

HUGH But Evelyn, who's going to actually be here, playing the scene with me? Tomorrow night?

EVELYN Kriston, of course.

CHRISSIE His agent's said he's still doing it.

EVELYN There. You see.

HUGH But...

EVELYN He just has a few issues to resolve.

HUGH He's not getting more money, is he?

EVELYN God, no. Look, don't worry Hugh, he'll be here. And you'll both be marvellous. But you'll be a bit more marvellous than him.

HUGH *steps out,* CHRISSIE *returns to her place and* WALTER *and* GEMMA *step back in.*

GEMMA "So, how did you find me Dad?

Long pause.

WALTER No. It's gone. Bollocks. Sorry everyone.

WALTER *steps out and* LINDA *steps back in.*

LINDA "*I* want to know about you, Linda. Me. And if you tell me...if you let me in... I won't share you with anyone."

GEMMA "I can't... I won't... I don't want anyone to..."

CHRISSIE Linda is abruptly stopped short, as the air is slapped out of her like a soufflé hurled onto wet arsefelt. Asphalt. She catches her breath like she is a butterfly in a net. Or maybe a moth?

LINDA "It's okay...baby..."

CHRISSIE Their lips, like two inexorable magnets, are drawn together and they kiss...as the lights fade to black.

EVELYN And...stop.

LINDA Is this *really* necessary Evelyn?

EVELYN Absolutely, it is. It's crucial to the integrity of the piece. Without this, nothing else makes sense.

GEMMA Alright. But the lights are going to go down quickly there, aren't they?

LINDA *steps out and* WALTER *steps back in with* GEMMA.

"So, how did you find me Dad?"

WALTER "It were..."

CHRISSIE The papers. I saw you in the papers.

WALTER I know! I was pausing dramatically. "I saw you in the papers. Soon as I saw you, in the papers, I knew, don't ask me how I did, but I did, I just knew it were you, Gemma."

GEMMA I'm Linda.

WALTER Bollocks!

> **WALTER** *steps out and* **HUGH** *and* **KRISTON** *step back in with* **GEMMA**.

EVELYN Welcome back, Kriston.

KRISTON Whatever. Let's just get this done, shall we.

> *They start the scene – tentatively and unhappily acting out the directions.*

"So then. We're all alone, Michael."

HUGH "Yes. I suppose we are. Lucian".

KRISTON "We won't be disturbed."

CHRISSIE He turns out the lights and then, in the reckless moonlight streaming through the window, he takes a dangerous step towards Michael.

HUGH "No. I suppose we won't."

CHRISSIE Standing on the tremulous brink, Michael allows Lucian to approach, right up him...*to* him... *Right up to him*. They kiss. Hungrily.

KRISTON Stop!!!

HUGH Stop!!!

CHRISSIE That's what it says in the script.

HUGH Evelyn, I'm not doing it.

KRISTON Me neither, man.

CHRISSIE's phone rings – she answers it and speaks quietly throughout the rest of the scene.

EVELYN No wait. I've got an idea. I can fix it.

GEMMA We don't know what we're doing. We're under-rehearsed.

EVELYN You've got exciting, fresh spontaneity.

LINDA *(to herself)* I hate Hugh.

EVELYN There's good creative tension.

KRISTON We don't have a set.

EVELYN What we do have is we have a fascinatingly blank canvas for the audience to let their unrestrained imaginations run across.

Beat.

WALTER Is it my line here?

EVELYN No!!! No, Walter! How?! How would it be your line?!

He stops. Takes a deep breath and composes himself.

I tell you, we're ready! Let's call this your dinner break, and we'll be back here in fifteen minutes. Ready to unleash Hildred McCann's Dark Heart of Art onto the world and give the audience a night in the theatre that they are never going to forget.

HUGH Or forgive.

EVELYN The show will go on!

CHRISSIE finishes her conversation and turns back to them.

CHRISSIE That was Hildred.

They all stare at her.

He's done a rewrite.

They all throw their scripts into the air.

Blackout.

INTERVAL

During the interval, there are Front of House announcements "This evening's premiere of the new play by Hildred McCann, Banksy Ain't Gay will begin in five minutes..."

ACT II

Performance

CHRISSIE *is heard over the PA system.*

CHRISSIE Ladies and gentlemen, in tonight's performance of Hildred McCann's new play, Banksy Ain't Gay, the part of "The Chorus" will be played by Mr Evelyn Mackintosh. Thank you.

The lights go down. A single spot comes up. EVELYN *is standing just outside it, terrified, dressed like a twat and carrying a heavy book. He shuffles into the light.*

EVELYN "I am Art. And 'Art' is the name but which...to which... but we give to the graffiti of our lives."

His single unscripted line over (and screwed up) he portentously opens the book. And reads:

"And this is the blank space – our canvas, to be filled with our art. Let there be light..."

The lights come up to reveal GEMMA.

"...and let there be music."

Music plays. Aretha Franklin singing **"YOU MAKE ME FEEL LIKE A NATURAL WOMAN".**

GEMMA *starts swaying and singing along to the music.*

"She dances. She sings. She is happy and secure. Safe in her home. Her arms tenderly envelop her own fleshy body like a sinewy, sensuous lover."

GEMMA *unhappily complies with this direction.*

"But then, like a pistol shot on an anvil!"

From offstage the front door bangs shut and abruptly kills the music stone dead. GEMMA *freezes and* HUGH *enters.*

GEMMA "You're home!"

HUGH "Yes. Home. Back where I started out this morning."

GEMMA "Oh Michael. It's *so* good to see you. Have you back home. With me. Again."

She hugs him tight to her.

"Home."

HUGH "Yes, Linda. I'm home."

HUGH *takes off his coat and looks for somewhere to hang it. Finally at a loss he thrusts it to* EVELYN.

GEMMA "How was your day?"

HUGH "My day?"

GEMMA "Yes. Your day. Teaching at that school."

HUGH Where I teach at?

GEMMA Yes. "Was it good? I want you to tell me about it. Everything. I want to hear it all."

HUGH *laughs.*

EVELYN Hear him laugh. Like a broken promise in an arid well.

HUGH *does his speech (which had been cut) totally throwing* GEMMA.

HUGH "My day was a day, a day like any other day." A day like a speech I've learnt and I'm going to do anyway sort of day. "It broke like an egg and smeared itself across the plate of the morning. The clock ticks on and the world races by, past me, busy and occupied – preoccupied and self-obsessed. Passing me by day by day by bye-bye day. And today? Today was just another day. Gone. Past. Another day older but none the wiser. Just another day closer to the end."

EVELYN "He picks up his coat...

EVELYN *hands* HUGH *his coat.*

"...But what is the point? So he puts it back down again."

HUGH *hands the coat back to* EVELYN.

GEMMA "I've got some fish. I thought we could have fish tonight. Would you like some fish?"

HUGH "Oh, Linda, what's the point of..."

Now GEMMA *does a speech that had been cut – totally pissing off* HUGH.

GEMMA "It was delivered. It arrived. Here. Today. In a van. It came here today in a van from the store. A man brought it to the door." Because you're not the only one who's lost a speech you'd learned.

Pause. She smiles at him.

HUGH "Oh Linda, what's..."

GEMMA "But I didn't let him in. I shouted through the letter box for him to just leave it on the step. And he did. The man in the van from the store left the fish on the step of the house. And when he went. Back in his van. I opened the door and brought the fish from the store on the step of the house inside. Inside our house. For you. Tonight."

HUGH *mouths* "You finished?" *before getting on with the lines.*

HUGH "Oh Linda, what's the point of fish? What's the point of all this?"

EVELYN "He wants, he yearns for anything but fish. Looking through the silent void of their love."

Her speech has thrown him and he is suddenly uncertain of his lines.

HUGH "I want to go..."

GEMMA "Out?"

HUGH Anywhere but here. But... "Yes. Yes, Linda, out. I want to go out."

GEMMA "Out? Away? From me?"

HUGH "Yes." *(Is this right?)* No?

EVELYN "Grasping her like a drowning man clutching a straw." *(Prompting)* He wants to take her.

GEMMA "Take me?"

HUGH Do I?

EVELYN With him.

GEMMA "Where?"

HUGH *struggles back on track.*

HUGH "Somewhere. Out there." Yes! "Where there's music and lights and laughter."

EVELYN "But see, see her eyes, her eyes as they widen like frightened holes in snow."

GEMMA "And people?"

HUGH Right. Them too. "Where there's lots of people."

GEMMA "No."

HUGH "Yes."

GEMMA "But, they'll...*look* at us."

HUGH "Let them. Let them all of them look at us. At the two of us together. Let's go out dancing, dancing in the spotlight, spinning in the limelight, like rabbits in the headlight."

GEMMA "We can't."

HUGH "Of course we can. Why can't we?"

GEMMA "We can't leave our house. Our lovely home."

HUGH "We'll be fine."

GEMMA "What if someone comes? Men. They'll penetrate our lovely home."

HUGH "We'll get a dog. He'll guard our home against the men."

GEMMA "We'll still be penetrated."

HUGH "We'll call him Rover."

GEMMA "I want it to be just us."

HUGH "Or Wags."

GEMMA "You and me and no one else."

HUGH "He'll be our best friend."

GEMMA "I don't want to be penetrated by a dog, Michael."

EVELYN "See, see him freeze, the rhythm dies and the moment is smashed like an egg."

MICHAEL "No. No, of course you don't. I can see that, Linda."

EVELYN "He turns..."

> **HUGH** *turns.*

> The other way.

> **HUGH** *turns the other way.*

> "...picks up his coat."

> **EVELYN** *hands* **HUGH** *the coat.*

> "And the moment hangs between them like a condemned man on a rope."

GEMMA "I'll make us some fish."

She hurries out.

EVELYN "And now see, see his anguish, twisting the coat in his tortured hands."

HUGH "Meee-ow!"

The lights slowly fade to inky blackness.

EVELYN "And listen. Hear in the black inkiness the sound of genius at work."

In the darkness, CHRISSIE *comes onto the stage, spraying a deodorant can around.*

"Spray cans hiss feverishly, like hectic snakes in a mattress, as a masterpiece blooms and is spattered onto the bricks of the wall of their lovely, safe home." Shit! Watch what you're doing with that, Chrissie!

He has a copped a load full in the face and starts choking violently.

The lights come up on EVELYN *on the floor clutching his face and* CHRISSIE *trying to help him. She looks up – trapped in the lights. There is nothing else to do but pick up the book that* EVELYN *has dropped. She is terrified but takes a deep breath and reads.*

CHRISSIE "The sun comes up on a new day. Listen."

Pause. Nothing is heard.

Pretend...that you can hear from outside... "the excited sound of an excited crowd of excited people intruding into this still room. And now see, see her as she enters, agitated like a lost child in a shopping mall."

GEMMA *enters. Seeing* CHRISSIE, *she is thrown but carries on.*

"Now see her open the closed curtains..."

GEMMA *mimes opening curtains one side of the stage.*

On stage right.

Lights flash on the opposite side to where GEMMA *is.*

"...and see the flashbulbs flash and hear the crowd fall silent."

From offstage, HUGH, LINDA *and* WALTER *holler gamely.*

"And feel, feel her panic as she shuts the curtains and cowers against the wall, clutching at her stomach like it is a sack of precious venom and screaming soundlessly."

GEMMA *croaks.*

GEMMA "Michael!"

HUGH *enters.*

During the following exchange, EVELYN *recovers and* CHRISSIE *gratefully leaves the stage.*

HUGH "What's going on?"

GEMMA "I'm being penetrated."

HUGH By a dog?

GEMMA No! "Out there. People. Looking in. In here. At me."

HUGH "You? Why?"

GEMMA "I don't know. Oh, make them go away. Please!"

HUGH "What the hell do they want?"

He moves towards the front door.

GEMMA "No! Please. Don't let them penetrate us."

She rushes into his arms.

HUGH "But what are they doing out there? What do they want?"

EVELYN "What do they want? What do they want? What do they want?"

This throws HUGH *and* GEMMA *who stare at him blankly.*
Clearly they don't know what they want.

Maybe it's on the news?

HUGH *and* GEMMA *look blank.*

On the radio!

The penny drops and HUGH *disentangles himself and*
crosses to the sideboard and mimes turning on the radio.
Immediately CHRISSIE *is heard, reading:*

CHRISSIE "...who died today. In other news, the...gorry-illa street
artist, Banksy, has struck again. His latest work appeared
quite suddenly overnight on the side of a quiet residential
house in a typical suburban street."

EVELYN "Quiet. Suburban. Street?"

CHRISSIE "The latest street masterpiece by the pseudonymous
graffiti artist, political activist, film director and painter
whose true identity is a closely guarded mystery has been
described as a spray-can painting of a man with a spray-
can, spray-can painting a spray-can painting of a man with
a spray-can who is spray-can painting a spray-can painting
of a man. With a spray-can."

HUGH "That's genius."

GEMMA "What can it mean?"

CHRISSIE "A large crowd has already gathered outside the
house, eagerly discussing the meaning behind this latest
daubing by the mysterious social commentator and satirist.
However the couple of the house on who's house the painting
has appeared have yet to make any public appearance or
statement."

There is a loud hammering at the door...

GEMMA "Who is it?"

EVELYN "Who is it?"

HUGH "Who is it?"

EVELYN "Listen. There is no reply."

Pause.

But more knocking.

There is more knocking at the door.

GEMMA "Make them go away."

HUGH "Go away!"

EVELYN "But see, see the letterbox open, like a dangerous mouth, ready to spit, cuss or bite."

LINDA *calls from offstage.*

LINDA "Hello? Is there anybody in there? Is there anyone at home?"

GEMMA "Who is it?"

HUGH "Who are you?"

LINDA "I'm from the press."

GEMMA "What do they want?"

LINDA "I want to talk to you about Banksy."

HUGH "What do you want?"

LINDA "I want to talk to you about Banksy." *(Beat)* Like I just said.

GEMMA "We don't know anything about that."

LINDA "You mean you don't know? It's here. The new Banksy is on the wall of your house."

EVELYN "And now see, see as Art strikes, strikes almost, but not quite, absolutely nothing like a viper in a baby-grow."

Blackout.

The lights come back up on the same scene a few minutes later. LINDA *has entered.*

LINDA "It was a good move, letting me in. Smart. Because you know, if it hadn't been me, it would have been someone else."

There is an uneasy beat. Whose line is it? Then they all three speak at once.

"And you wouldn't have wanted that."

GEMMA "What do you want with us?"

HUGH "Why wouldn't we have wanted someone else?"

Beat – just move on.

LINDA "It's a nice place you've got here."

They have skipped on a few pages and EVELYN *frantically has to find the page in his book.*

EVELYN "A chord is struck and the woman flutters like a hummingbird in a porcelain teacup."

GEMMA "Thank you. We like it."

LINDA "I like it. It's a 'home'. Immediately you walk in, you can tell. It has a story. Something to tell."

GEMMA "Does it?"

HUGH "What do you want?"

LINDA "To talk. About Banksy."

GEMMA "We don't know anything about him."

LINDA "No one does. That's why it's a story. He's a gwear-iya."

HUGH A what?

LINDA A gwear-iya! "Fighting society from behind a legend. Who is he? Or she? Banksy is no one and at the same time, everyone."

GEMMA "So what's this got to do with us?"

LINDA "It's up on your wall. You are now part of the legend."

HUGH "Why has he chosen us?"

GEMMA "Why has he sprayed his stuff all over us?"

GEMMA *can't disguise her distaste with this last line.*

LINDA "Fame is a random commodity these days. No one knows exactly where it will land next. Who it will touch. Or why?"

HUGH "But you're saying it has touched us?"

LINDA "You are touched."

HUGH "Do you hear that, Linda. We've been touched."

He reaches out to touch GEMMA.

EVELYN "But see, see her shrink from his touch in horrified horror."

LINDA "You're famous."

HUGH "Famous."

EVELYN "He has waited all his life to hear someone say these words to him."

GEMMA "No!"

EVELYN "And she has lived her entire life making sure she'd never have to hear those words."

LINDA "You are blank canvases and it's my job to fill you in. The world is waiting to see those empty spaces filled."

GEMMA "No! No! No! No! No! No! No!"

She rushes from the room.

LINDA "She's upset?"

HUGH "Yes." She missed one out. "But she'll come round. I expect."

From offstage GEMMA *yells defiantly.*

GEMMA No!!!

HUGH *moves close to* **LINDA**.

HUGH "So, what happens now?"

LINDA "Now?"

HUGH "Yes. What happens now? Between us?"

He moves uncomfortably close to her, eyeing her meaningfully. **LINDA** *simply stands, staring at him – still unfortunately attracted to him.*

EVELYN "See, see how, like a polished courtesan, she draws out a dining room chair, flips it round and straddles it, like a stallion, whilst at the same time, with her other hand, she produces a note pad from an inside pocket and flicks it open with skilful insouciance whilst drawing a pen from her breast pocket."

LINDA *gives* **EVELYN** *a "You must be kidding!" look as she breaks away from* **HUGH**.

LINDA Now, Hugh...*you*...you Michael... "You tell me everything."

Blackout.

Immediately **HUGH** *is picked up in a spotlight.*

HUGH "All my life I've waited for this moment. I've always known it would arrive. Fame? It's no big deal. I knew I was extraordinary and the fact I have no real talent for anything wasn't going to stop me being known. All I had to do was wait. Bide my time. Be patient. And then 'something' would happen. Something that was going to propel me up, like a firework, exploding into the lives of people. Ordinary people – not like me. I'm extra-ordinary. Up there, in people's lives is where I belong."

The lights flick back on.

EVELYN "But look. See. Who comes this way comes?"

KRISTON *is there, back to the audience. Slowly he turns around. He is wearing a blond wig and has suitably whited up his face. He is hating every moment of this.*

KRISTON "So...just who is spraying who here? Or whom? What's the deal? What are we *actually, fundamentally* looking at here? There's a man? Yes?"

EVELYN "Yes."

KRISTON "And the man is spray-can painting another man who is spray-can painting another man who is spray-can..." What the radio said. You know what I'm saying?

EVELYN Totally.

HUGH Absolutely.

KRISTON "Because we are looking at art by an artist who reveals himself...in disguise." That right? "Who is known for being *un*known. Glorying in his essential dark anonymity. A goorrilla bandit who works in the art of the illicit, who makes us complicit in his crimes through the very act of scrutiny. It's so terribly thrilling. But I'm sorry, I haven't properly introduced myself. Lucian Tonderei."

HUGH "The art dealer?"

EVELYN "Who could have guessed?"

KRISTON "I like to think of myself as a..." *(Beat)* Like I said earlier. I'm the guerrilla bandit.

HUGH Like Banksy?

KRISTON Yeah. Like him too. "You must be Michael."

HUGH "Yes. How did you..."

KRISTON "Oh, come now. *Everyone* knows you. The entire art world...the entire *nation* knows who you are. The man with the masterpiece up his back wall."

HUGH "You're too kind."

KRISTON "The moment I saw this Banksy I knew I had to come and see it for myself. And *then*, I saw you on the television... and I knew I had to come here and meet you...for myself." For some reason.

EVELYN "And see. See the very breath squeezed from his heart. He literally can't speak."

HUGH "I'm so happy to meet you."

EVELYN "But does."

Beat.

KRISTON "What an absolutely hideous room you have here. I love it."

EVELYN "And our 'hero' is suddenly flapping like a trout on the bank."

HUGH "Thank you. I think. It's..."

KRISTON "Yes?"

HUGH "...it's really more my..."

KRISTON "Your?"

HUGH "...partner..."

KRISTON "Partner?"

HUGH "...'s taste."

KRISTON "You have a partner."

HUGH "Yes. And it's really more her taste than mine."

EVELYN "He's as helpless as a rag doll in..."

But KRISTON *just powers over him.*

KRISTON "Her? Your partner, spouse, lover, significant other is a her?"

HUGH "Yes."

Pissed off, EVELYN *is determined to finish his line.*

EVELYN "Rag doll in a tumble dryer!"

KRISTON "Well, well, you *are* full of surprises Mr Michael."

He holds out a hand to HUGH *who takes it.*

"But all the same, it's utterly...delicious...to meet you."

EVELYN "And he holds his eyes in his" ...like a big gay boy..." before, finally after what seems an age but is actually only five seconds, he releases him. Abruptly."

KRISTON *breaks away from* HUGH.

KRISTON "Of course, you can't sell. It's out of the question."

HUGH "Sell?"

KRISTON "Out of the very question and it's crude to even contemplate selling your Banksy."

HUGH "Mine?"

KRISTON "Well, I assume this is your house. Yours and your... Mrs Michael."

HUGH "What do you mean, like?"

KRISTON "I mean, like, you own this house? You have a freehold on the property, deeds to the land, it is, under the common law of the land, free from restraining covenant, prima facie, res..."

EVELYN "Ipsa loquitur."

KRISTON Whatever... "Yours?"

HUGH "It's our house, yes."

KRISTON "Your house. Your floor, your roof, your...walls?"

HUGH "Yes. Of course."

KRISTON "Then the Banksy is...yours?"

HUGH "Yes."

EVELYN "Now, suddenly he catches where this stream is heading. And although, like a helpless, falling autumn leaf from a conker tree, he is caught in the swirling current, he tries to put his foot down and face up to his tormentor."

HUGH "It's not for sale."

EVELYN "But like a dead swan, the man is unflappable." And gay.

KRISTON "Of course it isn't. I told you. The *very* thought is unthinkable."

HUGH "We're not selling."

KRISTON "I know you're not. This is art from the underground. It is above the grubby base coin of mere...grubby commerce."

EVELYN "And beware his smile, like a treacherous lighthouse."

KRISTON "I'm so glad we understand each other. And we do understand each other. Don't we? Michael?"

HUGH "Yes. Yes, of course we do."

KRISTON "Call me Lucian."

HUGH "Lucian."

EVELYN "As slowly, slowly, slowly they rise and walk towards the inviting figure of the other, like a moth to a flame. Or is it a butterfly?"

As the lights fade to dark **HUGH** *and* **KRISTON** *make bloody sure they don't reach each other.*

In the black, a spotlight picks up **GEMMA**.

GEMMA "I always knew I was different. Not like the other children who peopled my childhood days. Their games were not my games. I tried... I wanted...but... I *knew*. I. Knew."

EVELYN "And watch, watch as she is shivered by the memories."

GEMMA "And they knew. My school chums. Playground pals... breaktime buddies...mates, cronies, companions...my... 'friends'...all of them...they could all see...sense...like young feral beasts, who scented blood, then set to running down their helpless prey. They could all see my...difference...smell my vulnerability and...relished in my weakness. And I was defenceless. I knew. They knew. And I knew they knew. And they knew I knew they knew. Like a man with a can, painting a man who is painting a man with a can, with a can, painting a man. Reflecting ourselves back on ourselves again and again and again. Until you don't know who you are...who you *really* are...standing alone, facing the pack who are staring you back..and then, they attack!"

EVELYN "No!"

GEMMA*'s performance goes completely over the top.*

GEMMA "The names! The stares! The glares, the looks, the sniggering, backhand, underhand, snide sniggers in the showers. The hours...hours alone, staring in the mirror, screaming at my body...tearing at the hated flesh...cutting... slashing...ripping at the despised carcass that encircled my misery. The sticks and stones that broke my bones and the words...the words that finally destroyed me."

Spent, she collapses to the floor.

EVELYN "And wracked by the fearsome remembrance, she shudders to an ugly orgasm of bad thoughts. Then comes the calm, drenching over her frame like a millpond of viscous self-loathing. And listen, listen when she speaks, she is empty, like a vessel with nothing in it."

GEMMA "I didn't hate them. There was no room for that. My loathing for myself was too encompassing. I couldn't fight them. Not until I had fought myself...my own, repugnant, detestable, abhorrent self...and won. And until I win that victory...until I feel like a Natural Woman...all I can do is hide. Hide inside."

The lights snap on and **GEMMA** *is sitting at the dining room table with* **LINDA** *who is scribbling in her pad. (She is still disconcerted from her last scene with* **HUGH**.*)*

LINDA "My God, Linda. You're so fascinating. So...deep. So... real. You have a story and the world is waiting to hear it."

GEMMA "No!"

LINDA "You're so...fascinating. So...deep. So...real."

GEMMA No.

LINDA *is lost on a loop.*

LINDA No?

GEMMA Well, yes, I am. But I'm also so enigmatic...

LINDA Yes! "You're so enigmatic, pragmatic and..." Pneumatic?

GEMMA Phlegmatic?

LINDA Yes.

GEMMA "No!"

LINDA Aren't you?

GEMMA No. "I'm no one. I don't even exist."

LINDA "No, Linda. You're so...fascinating. So...deep. So...real so..." Shit! Sorry.

She takes a breath and gets back on track.

"Since I first met you I felt...I don't know how I felt."

GEMMA "I've often felt that."

LINDA "I thought you would. You and I..."

GEMMA "What?"

LINDA "We have a connection. I feel there is more to you than there is to most women."

GEMMA "You would be surprised."

LINDA "Yes. Yes, I think I would be. You're so fascinating. So... deep. So...real...

EVELYN *comes to her rescue.*

EVELYN "And now see, look, watch as she is brought up short by something that has tripped her up like an emotional mantrap hidden under the green foliage of her own defences. And now glimpse, spot and observe, she is falling, tipping and tripping forward. She can't stop herself, like a runaway helter skelter."

LINDA "I'm sorry...please...go on...tell me more."

GEMMA "I don't know what else there is to say. I don't know what it is that you want me to say."

EVELYN And now her pad is pushed aside like a child's uneaten broccoli.

LINDA "I want you to tell me, Gemma."

GEMMA Linda. "Tell you what?"

LINDA "Tell me...everything."

GEMMA "I can't."

LINDA "Please."

EVELYN "There is a moment."

GEMMA "No."

EVELYN "And she breaks the moment like a porcelain swan hurled at a wall."

GEMMA "I can't."

EVELYN "A special wall?"

GEMMA "Please don't ask me."

EVELYN "With a Banksy sprayed across it like a genius cryptogram?"

LINDA "Please."

GEMMA "No."

LINDA "Please?"

GEMMA "No!"

LINDA "Please!"

GEMMA "No?"

LINDA "Please..."

GEMMA "...No."

LINDA "Why not?"

GEMMA "I can't. Don't you see? Don't you understand? I *can't* let them in."

LINDA "Who?"

GEMMA "Them. Out there. I can't let them inside me."

LINDA "This isn't for them. It's not for my readers."

GEMMA "But you're a journalist."

LINDA "To hell with that. All my life I've wanted to share the story. It's what I've lived for. But this...you...it's different. I want to know about you, Linda. Me. And if you tell me...if you let me in... I won't share you with anyone."

GEMMA "I can't... I won't... I don't want anyone to..."

LINDA "Penetrate?"

EVELYN "She has been stopped short. Like a sad clown slapped in the face by a custard pie of truth."

LINDA "It's okay...baby... I understand."

GEMMA "You...you do?"

LINDA "Of course I do. I'm like you. I am just like you."

GEMMA "Like me?"

LINDA "I won't penetrate you."

EVELYN "And see, see their lips, like two inexorable magnets, drawn together as they kiss..."

GEMMA "As the lights fade to black!"

The lights snap off – there is a beat then **LINDA** *appears in a spotlight. Reading from a crib sheet.*

LINDA "Read All About It! Exclusive! Banksy Reclusive Woman Speaks! 'I don't even exist' claims spray-can street art masterpiece Linda. Turn to pages three, four, five, six, seven, eight and nine for the full unexpurgated exposé... plus a special four-page, uncensored, full colour, centre page pull-out!"

EVELYN "And the moon rises and its blue light bathes the room."

After a couple of goes, the lighting state arrives and **HUGH** *and* **KRISTON** *enter.*

KRISTON "Thank you for coming to the opening, Michael."

HUGH "Thank you for asking me, Lucian."

KRISTON "He's a new artist, a pale interesting child who I've rather taken under my wing. I thought this latest work of his rather bold. Didn't you?"

HUGH "Yes. Although I'm not sure I completely understood it."

KRISTON "My dear, Michael. Art, isn't there to be understood. It's to make us *feel*. The exhibition tonight. What did it make you *feel*?"

HUGH "Confused?"

KRISTON "That's good."

HUGH "It made me wonder...why? Why he'd done it. I mean, what was the point?"

KRISTON "Art doesn't need a point."

HUGH "Yes. There must be some *reason*."

KRISTON "Of course there is."

HUGH "So what is it? Why?"

KRISTON "Well, in these works, obviously, what the artist has done is taken the..."

He searches for the line.

EVELYN "Homo-erotic, sub-textual iconography inherent in the 1970s all-in wrestling scene to a brave, audacious, extreme."

KRISTON That.

HUGH "And that's why he called it, 'Kendo Nagasaki Rams It Down Your Throat'?"

KRISTON "Exactly. He challenges us with work depicting proletarian cultural icons like Big Daddy, Giant Haystacks and…" The other one…

EVELYN "Mighty" John Quinn.

KRISTON Him. "…butt naked, like God intended and finally free to…" You know…

EVELYN "Lick, suck and sex each other without being judged by straight society, represented in these striking paintings by the sinister, shadowy figure of commentator, Kent Walton."

KRISTON That.

Pause.

HUGH "My gran always used to watch it on Saturday afternoons."

KRISTON "It must have brought back such memories."

HUGH "It's certainly made me think of her in a different light."

KRISTON "It's *changed* you?"

HUGH "Yes, I suppose it has."

KRISTON "Then that, Michael, is what 'art' is for. You don't get out much, do you? You should. You're much better. When you're…out."

EVELYN "And look, look at the look that he looks at him. And listen, listen to hear the something unspoken, desperate to be said but knowing that they don't have the words. Not yet."

HUGH "Thank you."

KRISTON "It's my..."

EVELYN *charges in with the line.*

EVELYN Burning deep into him with his big gay homosexual eyes.

KRISTON "...pleasure."

EVELYN "And then, in the reckless moonlight streaming through the window, they take a another dangerous step towards each other."

HUGH *and* **KRISTON** *resolutely do not move.*

Closer and closer.

They aren't playing along.

Until they stand on a tremulous brink!

They make a tentative and half-hearted stab at an embrace.

"And finally they kiss. Hungrily. Clawing at each other's shoulders. And backs. And buttocks."

They break away from each other.

KRISTON Forget it, man.

EVELYN What? Look, just pretend.

HUGH Let's just move on, Evelyn.

EVELYN What is your problem, Hugh?

HUGH *My* problem!?

EVELYN Is it your racism?

KRISTON What racism? I'm white, remember?

HUGH I just don't think it's artistically justified.

KRISTON I just don't dig kissing guys.

EVELYN You two are *so* repressed!

KRISTON How about we tear you a new asshole! Is that liberated enough for you, Eve-er-lyn?

Before this situation escalates, **CHRISSIE** *appears at the back of the stage, holding a book and reading:*

CHRISSIE "And suddenly, the lights click on, and Linda is standing at the bedroom door."

GEMMA *appears in the doorway.*

GEMMA "Michael, is that you? I thought I heard voices and..."

CHRISSIE "And see, see how she stops dead in frozen shock at the sight of Michael and Lucian."

EVELYN Deeply snogging each other's faces.

GEMMA "Michael!"

EVELYN With tongues.

HUGH "Linda!"

GEMMA "Michael? Who is this...man?"

KRISTON "I'm Lucian. I'm Michael's new friend."

EVELYN In inverted commas.

CHRISSIE "Look warmly at the warm look, but with a malicious hint of nasty, he tosses at the sick-looking Michael."

KRISTON "I'm going to buy your Banksy."

GEMMA "What? I don't understand. Michael?"

HUGH "I haven't said we're selling it."

KRISTON "Not yet maybe."

CHRISSIE "He gently strokes Michael's frozen cheek as he passes him on the way out."

KRISTON *and* **HUGH** *do an elaborate high five as they pass.*

KRISTON "I'll see myself out."

EVELYN "And as soft as an elf on butter, he drifts out of the door." And the play.

KRISTON *flips the bird as he leaves.*

CHRISSIE "Leaving a moment. Feel, feel the moment..."

EVELYN "Hanging like icicles between them."

CHRISSIE "Until..."

EVELYN "...finally..."

GEMMA "Where have you gone?"

HUGH "Out."

GEMMA "From me? Oh... Michael..."

CHRISSIE "There are no more words."

EVELYN "He stares helplessly at her."

CHRISSIE "Who stares back at him. We can feel their hearts breaking in tandem. And now, after what feels like years..."

EVELYN "But is actually fourteen seconds..."

CHRISSIE "Joe appears in the doorway."

WALTER *enters from the wrong place.*

WALTER "Kevin?"

GEMMA *and* **HUGH** *wheel around.*

HUGH "What?"

WALTER "Kevin?"

GEMMA "Dad?"

HUGH "Who?"

GEMMA "This is my dad."

WALTER "KEVIN!"

HUGH "Who?"

WALTER *rushes to* GEMMA.

WALTER "This is my son!"

EVELYN "He clasps her to him like he will never let her go again."

CHRISSIE "She clasps at him, finally at home in Daddy's strong arms."

HUGH "No! Linda! No! No! No!!!"

He rushes out.

The lights click off.

They slowly fade up again on GEMMA *and* WALTER, *sitting drinking tea.*

From offstage HUGH *bellows.*

No!!!

GEMMA "So, how did you find me, Dad?"

There is a pause, then, resigned, EVELYN *passes the book to* WALTER *who reads.*

WALTER "It were the papers. I saw you in the papers. Soon as I saw you, in the papers, I knew, don't ask me how I did, but I did, I just knew it were you, Kevin."

He passes the book back.

Thanks.

GEMMA "Linda."

WALTER "What?"

GEMMA "I'm Linda now, Dad."

WALTER "Oh. Yes. I see. 'Course you are. I was forgetting."

EVELYN "And feel, feel the awkward silence like an ill-fitting macintosh on a hunch-backed vicar."

WALTER "So you've had a..." you know...

GEMMA Sex change?

WALTER Yes.

GEMMA Yes.

WALTER And that was your...?

GEMMA Husband? Yes.

CHRISSIE Pause.

> **EVELYN** *gives her a look – she needn't have said that.*

WALTER So how come he's never noticed?

GEMMA Oh, I don't know.

> *Long pause until finally...*

CHRISSIE Pause over.

GEMMA "Why did you come here, Dad?"

WALTER "I wanted to see you. I've *needed* to see you. To tell you..."

EVELYN "Feel him."

CHRISSIE "Feel him old and vulnerable and confused."

EVELYN "And beginning to crack?"

WALTER "I'm so sorry. I know you blame me, I should have been different. I drove you away, I know that. But it weren't my fault. I'm a man and I wanted a son. I wanted you to like football and guns and have a bike with a crossbar. Drink beer, laugh at farts, sit with your legs apart on the bus, scratch, sniff, get a girl pregnant, go to war, get yourself killed and make me proud. Be a man! And it were like the more I tried to make you into what I wanted you to be, the more you retreated and hid from me. Because as I looked at you, it were like I were a man looking at... I don't know... some sort of...painting...of a man painting..."

As they all feared, **WALTER** *has gone off-piste. It's now all hands on deck to pull him through.*

EVELYN A painting of a painted man painting a painting of a man painting.

WALTER That were it. Now, where were I?

CHRISSIE Realising you were never looking at what you actually saw in front of your own blind eyes. A beautiful daughter.

WALTER I thought she was my son.

CHRISSIE She was.

EVELYN Sort of.

WALTER I'm lost.

GEMMA Oh... Dad.

WALTER What? Oh. Yes. Your mum. Now, she never forgave me. I think. Yes, there's something now about how the cancer finally took her...and her giving me a look...which is like a painting of a painting of a...? No! We've done that... Now... Got it... "It's like her look is like the look what you're giving me now...because you look like her...your mum...because you're now a woman"...and...and...

EVELYN His unravelment is almost complete.

WALTER "I've been so lonely!" That's it.

And we're back on track...for the moment.

CHRISSIE "And now the tears. Held back for so many years..."

EVELYN "Disguised by male bravado, anger and alcohol, the tears have finally come."

WALTER Oh, Christ, I've got to cry now.

He starts scrunching his face up.

GEMMA "Dad..."

WALTER Hang on. Nearly there.

GEMMA "Dad."

Pause.

Please.

WALTER "What?"

GEMMA "Say something? Like you're so sorry."

WALTER "Am I?"

GEMMA "Yes. You're sorry for everything. You always knew I were what I were but you couldn't even allow yourself to accept that what I was was acceptable. You don't know why but you couldn't let yourself just tell me how much you loved your son."

WALTER Not daughter?

GEMMA No, son!

WALTER I give up.

GEMMA "You was a fool to let me hide myself away from you like I did. To cause me all the hurt and pain like what you did. You know that and you can never forgive yourself for that. And now, you've come back to ask me for another chance because you're so lonely and you've got no one."

WALTER That was very good.

GEMMA "Daddy..."

She kneels down with him and enfolds her arms around him.

WALTER Is this the bit where we...

GEMMA "Don't upset yourself so."

EVELYN "He's missed his daughter."

CHRISSIE "Missed his son."

EVELYN "He's missed her mum."

CHRISSIE "He's so very alone."

GEMMA "It's alright, Dad. I'm here. And I forgive you. We're together now."

EVELYN "See, see her gently stroke his hair, caressingly soothing and comforting."

CHRISSIE starts to get increasingly uneasy about this next bit. As does GEMMA having to act it out.

CHRISSIE "See, see his strong, gnarly hands reach out for her, feeling her body, slowly discovering her womanliness."

EVELYN "Oh...it's been so long...so long..."

GEMMA "It's alright, Dad. It's you and me."

CHRISSIE "She kisses him kindly."

EVELYN "He kisses her back, gratefully."

CHRISSIE "She kisses him invitingly."

EVELYN "He kisses her achingly."

CHRISSIE "They kiss each other hungrily?"

EVELYN "He claws at her with an increasingly desperate passion that she finds herself responding to."

GEMMA Do I have to?

WALTER Oh Kevin. You've got fabulous tits!

EVELYN "Scrabbling at each other, they desperately tear at each other's clothing as they roll together behind the sofa."

As there isn't a sofa, CHRISSIE does her best to shield them.

CHRISSIE And the lights fade! Quickly!!!

The lights snap off and in the darkness we hear GEMMA disentangling herself from WALTER (who's put his back out).

Then...

GEMMA "I don't know what came over me. It was wrong. I knew it was wrong, it felt wrong, there was nothing about it that was right. But I had no control. At that very moment it felt...like I was being painted. By a man. A man who was being painted by a man who was just a painting by another man...who was being painted. By a man..." Whatever. "Like it has been all my life. Like I have spent all my life...absent."

The lights slowly come up. WALTER *is lying with a knife sticking out of his chest.* GEMMA *is standing beside him. Blood spattered. Behind her, looking on in shocked tableaux are* HUGH, LINDA *and* KRISTON *(who has got his bag ready to go).*

"He penetrated me. So I penetrated him. But now finally it is over. At last I know what it is I have to do."

CHRISSIE "See, see her pick up the sledgehammer on the sideboard." *(Beat)* Really?

There is a sledgehammer and GEMMA *picks it up, struggling with its weight.*

GEMMA "Banksy has destroyed my life. Banksy has destroyed my home. Banksy has exposed, uncovered and laid me bare. Banksy has destroyed me. Now I am going to destroy Banksy."

She tries to brandish the sledgehammer, high above her head and nearly falls off the stage.

KRISTON "No!"

LINDA "Linda!"

HUGH "Think of the fame!"

KRISTON "Think of the art!"

LINDA "Think of the story!"

WALTER "Think of yourself."

With enormous effort he pushes himself up, as the life ebbs from him.

"If you destroy Banksy, you'll destroy yourself."

GEMMA "But... I don't understand."

WALTER "I think you do. You've always known."

GEMMA "Known what?"

WALTER "What it's taken me all my life to find out. What I finally know now. And that it's you."

GEMMA "Me?"

HUGH "Her?"

LINDA "Who?"

KRISTON What?

GEMMA "You mean?"

WALTER "Yes...my *son*. Daughter. It's you. You are Banksy."

He dies. Then remembers to raise his fist in salute.

GEMMA "I am Banksy!"

She raises her fist in salute. Behind her, HUGH's *fist goes up.*

HUGH "No! I am Banksy!"

Next to him KRISTON *raises his defiant fist.*

KRISTON "It's me! I am Banksy!"

Then LINDA *raises her fist.*

LINDA "I'm Banksy!"

CHRISSIE *and* EVELYN *address the audience.*

CHRISSIE "You!"

EVELYN "You are Banksy!"

ALL We!! *WE ARE BANKSY*!!

They hold the pose.

Then...

CHRISSIE "The end."

The cast collapse into each other's arms and... Blackout.

PROPERTY LIST

ACT I

Marking tape on the floor
Lots and lots of scripts for all the cast
Pencils for all the cast
Smartphone for **Chrissie**
Newspaper with crossword for **Walter**
Thermos of tea for **Gemma** and **Linda**
Animal carrying cage for **Chrissie**
Damp sweatshirt for **Hugh**

ACT II

Heavy book for **Evelyn**
Overcoat for **Hugh**
Aerosol cans for **Chrissie**
Reporters pad and pen for **Linda**
Crib sheets with her lines on it for **Linda**
Book for **Chrissie**
Tea cups for **Gemma** and **Walter**
Knife for **Walter**
Packed suitcase for **Kriston**
Sledgehammer for **Gemma**

LIGHTING AND SOUND/EFFECTS

ACT I

Blackout (p64)

ACT II

Sound/Effects

During the interval, there are Front of House announcements
"This Evening's Premiere of the new play by Hildred McCann,
Banksy Ain't Gay will begin in 5 minutes..." (p65)
Chrissie is heard over the PA system (p66)
Music plays. Aretha Franklin singing "YOU MAKE ME FEEL
LIKE A NATURAL WOMAN" (p66)
From offstage the front door bangs shut and abruptly kills the
music stone dead (p67)
There is a loud hammering at the door...(p73)
There is more knocking at the door (p74)

Lighting

The lights go down. A single spot comes up (p66)
The lights come up to reveal Gemma (p6)
The lights slowly fade to inky blackness (p71)
Lights flash on the opposite side to where Gemma is (p72)
Blackout (p74)
The lights come back up on the same scene a few minutes
later (p75)
Spotlight (p77)
The lights flick back on (p77)
As the lights fade to dark (p81)
In the black, a spotlight picks up Gemma (p81)
The lights snap off – there is a beat then Linda appears in a
spotlight (p86)
The lighting state arrives (p86)
The lights click off (p91)
They slowly fade up (p91)
The lights snap off (p95)
The lights slowly come up (p96)

Blackout (p98)

THIS
IS
NOT
THE
END

Lightning Source UK Ltd.
Milton Keynes UK
UKHW02f1600110418
320862UK00006B/734/P